Costume Society of America Series
Phyllis A. Specht, Series Editor

The Sunbonnet

Courtesy of the Texas Fashion Collection, College of Visual Arts,
University of North Texas.

The
Sunbonnet
An American
Icon in
Texas

Rebecca Jumper Matheson

Texas Tech University Press

This book is typeset in Monotype Joanna. The paper used in this book meets the minimum requirements of ANSI/NISO Z39.48-1992 (R1997). ∞

Designed by Kasey McBeath

Library of Congress Cataloging-in-Publication Data

Matheson, Rebecca Jumper, 1975–
    The sunbonnet : an American icon in Texas / Rebecca Jumper Matheson.
        p. cm. — (Costume society of America series)
    Includes bibliographical references and index.
    Summary: "This first book-length history of the American sunbonnet, which persisted as folk dress late into the twentieth century, discusses what the sunbonnet reveals about American fashion, culture, ideals, and class- and race-related issues. Details sunbonnet construction, care, and design differences; includes oral histories and a variety of visual primary sources"—Provided by publisher.
    ISBN 978-0-89672-665-9 (pbk. : alk. paper) 1. Women's hats—Texas—History.
I. Title.
    GT2110.M265 2009
    391.4'3—dc22   2009022895
Printed in the United States of America
09   10   11   12   13   14   15   16   17 / 9   8   7   6   5   4   3   2   1

Texas Tech University Press | Box 41037 | Lubbock, Texas 79409-1037 USA
800.832.4042 | ttup@ttu.edu | www.ttup.ttu.edu

Contents

Contents

viii

Illustrations

Figures

Patterns

Color Plates (following page 130)

★ ★ ★

Acknowledgments

So many people have helped me in bringing this book to fruition; I am grateful for their assistance and encouragement. Many thanks to Dr. Lourdes Font, my advisor on the original Fashion Institute of Technology master's thesis that grew into this book; at the Metropolitan Museum of Art, Harold Koda, Christine Paulocik, Elizabeth Bryan, Jessica Reagan, and Joyce Fung in the Costume Institute, as well as museum photographer Karin Willis and Deanna Cross of the Image Library; at the Texas Fashion Collection, Myra Walker, Heather Imholt, and photographer Andrea Hoback; at the Museum at Texas Tech University, Mei Campbell, Matt Renick, and photographer Bill Mueller; at Condé Nast, Marianne Brown, Leigh Montville, Dawn Lucas, and Gretchen Fenston; at the Maryland

Historical Society, Chris Becker; at the Library of Congress, Mark Lewis; at the Texas AgriLife Extension Service, Bill McConnell and Elizabeth Gregory North. Thanks also to Kristen Stewart who created the poke-style sunbonnet pattern for the appendix of this book and did technical illustrations. Thank you to my copyeditor, Katherine Hinkebein. A special thank-you to editor-in-chief Judith Keeling, as well as Phyllis Specht, Barbara Werden, Sarah Hays, Jada Von-Tungeln, Karen Medlin, Joanna Conrad, and everyone at Texas Tech University Press.

I am deeply grateful to those who shared sunbonnet information with me. Narrators Faye Rusk, Louise Rusk, Minnie Lee Skelton, and Julia Brazil, as well as Eileen Johnson, provided invaluable insights. Star Caldwell and Joanne W. Thompson generously shared patterns. Thank you all!

On a very personal level, thank you to Jack and Dana Jumper and Rachel Leah Jumper for encouragement through the years. I could not have undertaken this project without the love and tremendous support of Dan Matheson, and I could not have completed it without the precocious forbearance of Elizabeth Grace Matheson. Thank you, thank you Team Matheson. Above all, all glory to God, apart from whom I can do nothing.

The Sunbonnet

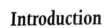

Introduction

What is your first association with the word *sunbonnet*? Do you picture a scene from the *Little House on the Prairie* television program, a Civil War reenactment, or perhaps a Sunbonnet Sue quilt square? Let me tell you a memory . . .

The year was 1929, and the Piney Woods of East Texas had been clear cut into great bald patches of red earth and cotton plants. In the middle of one of these cotton fields a teenager named Louise was deftly wielding her hoe against the never-ending onslaught of insidious weeds. Chop, chop, chop! Despite the strangulating heat, Louise's outfit covered her from head to foot: she wore a long-sleeved shirt under her jaunty striped overalls, and her fashionable bobbed hair was covered by her capacious slat sunbonnet.

As she worked her way down the row, she was getting closer to the fence line and the road beyond, where a mule-driven wagon was rattling its approach. Louise was the baby of her family, "petted" and spoiled by the rest of her kin ever since her mother had died when she was a toddler. But she, like everyone else, had to chop cotton. Truth be told, she liked being outside, liked working in the fields better than the indoor work that her older sister supervised.

It was so humid out this morning that it was already becoming unbearable, with hours to go before the dinner bell would welcome her to shade and a meal. A drop of perspiration began to crawl down the back of Louise's scalp, creepy-itchy as a June bug catching at your hair. Louise paused in her work, leaned the hoe in the crook of her arm, and took off her slat bonnet for just a moment, just long enough to shake out the soft, short layers of her bob. She immediately put the bonnet back on, retying it smartly under her chin. As she did, she looked back toward the road. The wagon was passing by, and the driver, a young man not much older than herself, was watching her intently.

The young man, in the way of Romantic young men, was busy deciding that Louise was the most beautiful woman he had ever seen; in fact, that it was love at first sight. He was already making up his mind to marry her . . . and one day he would.

At least this is the way I imagine it must have been. Louise was my grandmother, and this story of how my grandfather Loinel saw her working in the field and fell in "love at first sight" was one I grew up hearing. She would certainly have been wearing her slat sunbonnet, but whether or not she took it off for a moment I don't know, and it is now too late to ask. Louise passed away on June 15, 2008. My grandmother's lifelong practice of wearing sunbonnets and her spirit of dogged determination certainly sparked my interest in the sunbonnet as both object and symbol, and they were ultimately the inspiration for this book.

Some of my earliest childhood memories are of playing quietly with my corncob dolls in the shade of my grandmother's fig and pecan trees, dressing my "babies" in clothes fashioned from Louise's scrap basket while she worked diligently in her vegetable garden. The East Texas sun would beat down, the iron-rich red earth roasting beneath it. This was the late 1970s. I would play in a cotton sundress, but Louise never ventured out into the sun without a long-sleeved shirt, long trousers, gardening gloves, and one great essential: her (poke-style in later years) cotton sunbonnet.

Just as my father's cowboy hat symbolized for me the spirit of the Texas man, so my grandmother's sunbonnet became my icon of Texas womanhood. But while my father understood that his cowboy hat signified difference, and that wearing it was certainly a declaration of identity when traveling (whether in New Delhi or New York), my grandmother wore her sunbonnet unself-consciously. To her, the sunbonnet was simply an item of utility, not a marker of identity.

Enter any Texas store selling western wear—whether the large complex geared toward tourists, the department-type store such as Baskin's, or the local feed store—and a selection of cowboy hats is sure to be plentiful, in styles both for men and women. But it is rare to find sunbonnets for sale outside of living history museum gift shops. Why is it that the sunbonnet, a garment so prevalent in the history of American rural life and Manifest Destiny–driven settlement patterns, seemingly has no place in contemporary western clothing?

I believe the omission can be traced to prevailing American myth making and popular ways of viewing our history. For example, images of an American past have been created and shaped by Hollywood film and television, which glorified the John Wayne heroes in their cowboy hats, but confined images of sunbonnet wearers to the likes of Scarlett O'Hara and her sisters laboring in the fields in post–Civil War poverty. The cowboy hat is not inherently more glamorous than the sunbonnet; it simply has had a better public relations team. In fact, the coonskin cap craze of 1954–1955 perfectly illustrates how a humble frontier accessory could be instantly elevated to stardom. After the segment *Davy Crockett* aired on Walt Disney's television program *Disneyland* in December 1954, children clamored for all things Crockett . . . and ten million coonskin caps were sold.[1] Again, the male hero's dress was admired and emulated.

But what of the sunbonnet? I believe it has been overlooked, just as the women who wore sunbonnets have been underrepresented on the pages of history. This book attempts to reclaim a bit of ground for the heroines of the sunbonnet—hardworking women whose lives were delineated not in battles won or lost but in rows of cotton chopped, bushels of vegetables grown and canned, miles of frontier trail traveled, lives of children birthed. In my mind today, as both a fashion historian and an interested observer, the sunbonnet occupies a special place in the history of working dress in the United States.

R. Turner Wilcox defines the bonnet as a "hood-shaped hat which ties under the chin."[2] The sunbonnet is a cloth bonnet, often worn for outdoor work, which provides shade through a stiffened brim protecting the face, a soft crown over the head, and a "tail" covering the neck (Fig. 1). Although the sunbonnet is an easily recognizable symbol of American pioneer life, little research has focused on this once ubiquitous accessory. Most current literature on sunbonnets discusses them only within the context of a wider discourse on folklore and folk dress, frontier or pioneer dress, or general millinery. Even less exists in the literature of dress to explain why the sunbonnet, as an example of agricultural working dress design, was so successful that it persisted throughout the twentieth century in pockets of the rural South, including East Texas.[3] (For the purposes of this book, the "South" includes states from Virginia to Texas. The areas of East Texas discussed in this book are most closely culturally aligned with the upland/inland regions of Louisiana, Mississippi, Alabama, and Georgia.)

This book endeavors to fill this vacuum and to establish the American sunbonnet as more than just a curiosity of folk dress. By analyzing who wore the sunbonnet, when it was worn, why it was worn, how it was made, what materials were used to construct it, and differences in sunbonnet design, we will begin to see the sunbonnet take shape as an important expression of American fashion history and material culture. From this vantage point, we will be prepared to discuss what the sunbonnet reveals about American culture.

This project was percolating in my mind before I began pursuing my master's degree at the Fashion Institute of Technology in New York City in 2003. After spending a few years living overseas in Australia, and then back in the United States in the metropolis of New York, I had a fuller sense of how interesting it really was that there were at least a few women still alive in East Texas who continued to wear sunbonnets for work gear. This generation of women, in their late eighties or early nineties at the turn of the millennium, had worn sunbonnets as a matter of course in their

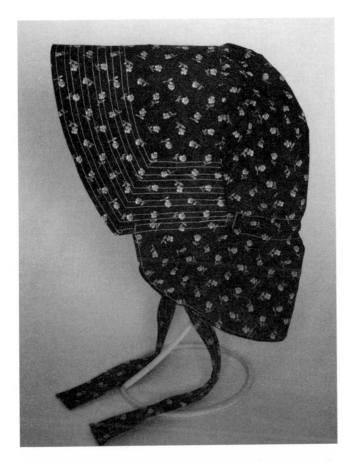

Fig. 1. Louise Jenkins Rusk's black with pink floral print poke-
style sunbonnet, with quilting following the brim silhouette.
c. 2000. This was an everyday bonnet that hung on the peg by
her back door until her death in 2008. Author's collection.
Photograph by the author.

youth. Some continued to wear this anachronistic garment throughout the twentieth century, others discarded it as the years went by. But as I began my graduate work, I had a sense that telling the story of the sunbonnet was important, and if I wanted to include the insights of this last generation (apart from those women who wear sunbonnets for religious reasons) of American sunbonnet wearers, I would need to act quickly.

Published secondary sources on the sunbonnet are relatively few and far between, but I cobbled together a bibliography, discovering multidisciplinary bits of information about the sunbonnet here and there. The foundation of my research used the historical method to consider the history of sunbonnet wear in the context of changing American society. I searched for documentary evidence, reading newspaper articles and memoirs of nineteenth-century sunbonnet wearers, investigating nineteenth-century mail-order catalogs' sunbonnet offerings.

The sunbonnet's appearance in literature further elucidates its meanings; as Aileen Ribeiro suggests, "literature conveys emotions and feelings about clothes that can highlight character and further the plot of a play or novel; at times . . . fashion itself can be said to produce fiction."[4] This book looks to examples of fiction that describe sunbonnets as a source of information about the bonnets themselves, as well as the ways in which they were perceived.

Additionally, material culture methodology is used to examine objects and explain their meanings within American culture. Material culture methodology, once the domain of anthropologists and archaeologists but now used by scholars in many fields, means studying things in order to understand people.[5] In my research I traveled to look at extant sunbonnets in various collections, in the hope of understanding more about the people who wore sunbonnets through contemplating the garments themselves. The theoretical framework of this book includes the work of Jules David Prown, as I attempt to step back and see what the sunbonnet's form implies about the culture that created it.[6] If I came from outer space and landed in Louise's father's cotton field in 1929, what would the form of Louise's slat sunbonnet tell me about her culture and beliefs? Why was it so important to stay out of the sun?

Oral history methodology was also extremely important in order to include the experiences of actual sunbonnet wearers, like my grandmother. The oral history methodology in this book looks to the "Principles and Standards of the Oral History Association."[7] Oral history is especially useful in studying rural working dress because this methodology allows the researcher to discover previously undocumented aspects of everyday dress, uncover local and specific information, and follow up immediately with questions on unclear issues.[8] As a fashion historian, I have researched many fashion designers who left wonderful, entertaining memoirs, as over-the-top as you would expect from someone who sold fantasy as well as clothing. But most of the women who wore sunbonnets as part of their daily work attire will never write a memoir; if the information is to be recorded, someone will have to take the initiative to seek it out. I found these women had great memories regarding their clothing. As George Ewart Evans notes, "In my experience the older generations, especially perhaps in the countryside, are greatly interested in dress because each change in fashion represented a milestone in their lives. . . . The minutest detail—especially the behavior and dress of your neighbors—was registered with surprising accuracy."[9] Oral history is also useful for discovering evidence of dress practices persisting past the period when they are widely presumed to have disappeared.[10]

In my preliminary research on the sunbonnet, I discovered that much of the available published information on Texas sunbonnets quoted (sometimes without citation) two short oral history interviews conducted by high school students and published in *The Loblolly Book* in 1983![11] It immediately became clear to me that analyzing existing primary materials would not be sufficient to even begin to tell the story of the American sunbonnet. It was imperative that I seek out fresh oral history sources and record them as quickly as possible.

In spring 2004 I was able to locate four East Texas sunbonnet wearers who were willing to participate in microtape recorded oral history interviews specifically on the subject of sunbonnets, as well as one sunbonnet seller who did not participate in a named, taped interview, but who did share information with me. I refer to these women throughout the text as "narrators." The women I interviewed personally will be identified using their first names to distinguish them from previously published sources: Louise, Faye, Minnie Lee, Julia, Eileen.[12] [For brief biographical information on Louise, Faye, Minnie Lee, and Julia, see Chapter 10: The Oral Histories; for more on Eileen, see Chapter 9: Decline (and Revival?) of the Sunbonnet.] My sense of urgency was also well-founded: in the time that has elapsed since I began my research and completed my first oral history interviews, most of my wonderful and spirited narrators have already passed away.

I would also have loved to have gotten the perspective of male narrators and their perceptions of the sunbonnet as a garment worn by women they knew. However, as a visit to my family cemetery in East Texas attests, while quite a few of the women of that generation have survived into their nineties, few men enjoyed the same long life span. I am left wondering what the "menfolk" saw and thought when they looked at women, faces shaded by the sunbonnet.

As the title of this book suggests, my approach is weighted toward sources of information from Texas, even as I acknowledge the importance of sunbonnets across the United States, as well as internationally. This is simply because these were the sources best known and available to this researcher; there are so many other regions in which local sunbonnets and sunbonnet wearers are deserving of attention. For example, I also received valuable written primary source information, as well as patterns, from the home economist Joanne W. Thompson of Arkansas, and the early twentieth-century photographs I studied show women in other regions of the South and the West. However, even where I primarily rely on findings from one area, I hope both to be able to draw some broader generalizations and to encourage others to take up this area of study in their region.

The sunbonnet was worn in areas outside the United States; for instance, sunbonnets were worn by working-class women in some rural areas of England in the nineteenth and early twentieth centuries.[13] Closer to home, rural Canadian women in the nineteenth century also wore sunbonnets.[14] However, because the sunbonnet, like the cowboy hat, took on a unique symbolic role in the United States, this volume mainly focuses on American sunbonnets and sunbonnet wearers, incorporating a few international sources where they shed light on American practices as well.

How this American icon came to survive in Texas and what its story reveals about frontier women and American culture must be understood first through exploring the sunbonnet's place in the history of millinery and fashion. In Chapter 1 I will consider other forms of millinery related to the sunbonnet; Chapters 2 and 3 trace the sunbonnet as we know it through the nineteenth century to the turn of the twentieth century. My sunbonnet narrators were born in the second decade of the twentieth century, so from the 'teens and twenties forward, their voices of personal experience form the core of this book's discussion of the sunbonnet in twentieth-century Texas.

Before attempting to discuss the history of the sunbonnet, some terminology must be established. For many twentieth-century sunbonnet wearers, the word *bonnet* is used interchangeably with *sunbonnet*.[15] To avoid confusion with fashionable bonnets, such as those worn for much of the nineteenth century, this book will use the general term *sunbonnet* wherever practical. However, the reader will note that in the oral history interview transcripts that appear in Chapter 10, reference is more often made simply to *bonnets*, in keeping with the language comfortably used by the narrators.

There are two main categories of sunbonnet: the poke-style sunbonnet, such as the one I remember my grandmother Louise wearing later in her life (1970s–2000s), and the slat sunbonnet, which she wore in the early twentieth-century days of hand-picked cotton production.[16] Throughout this book, the two types of sunbonnets will be compared and contrasted in terms of structure, construction methods, and materials, as well as design elements.

There seems to be a consensus that the part of the sunbonnet that extends past the face to create shade is called the brim, and that the fabric piece over the top of the head is the crown.[17] Removable, usually rectangular, pieces (primarily wood or cardboard) that give firmness to a brim may be called slats or staves. The twentieth-century East Texas wearers usually call these pieces staves.[18] Layers of fabric, interfacing, or other nonremovable materials sewn into the brim of a sunbonnet to give it firmness are often termed stiffening. Pieces of fabric that extend from the inside of the sunbonnet to tie under the chin, or are sewn across the back of the neck, are simply called ties.[19]

A crucial part of the everyday sunbonnet is the length of material that flows down from the crown to cover the wearer's neck. In works previously published by folklorist Janet K. Jeffery and fashion historian Betty J. Mills, this part is often called the bavolet, in keeping with the terminology used for fashionable bonnets of the nineteenth century, or occasionally the cape, curtain, or neck ruffle.[20] However, twentieth-century sunbonnet wearers of East Texas agree that this part of the sunbonnet is called the tail.[21] In deference to the authority of the women who have spent so many days of their lives wearing a sunbonnet, this book will refer to a sunbonnet's neck covering as the tail, while using the term bavolet when discussing the corresponding component in other forms of headgear.

The sunbonnet is a garment that has been worn throughout the period of American nationhood. This humble piece of millinery is more than just a pioneer accessory; it has played an important role in the realm of rural American dress for generations. It is emblematic of the United States as an agrarian society: the sunbonnet's disappearance parallels American urbanization in the twentieth century.

1

Fashionable Millinery Related to the Sunbonnet

The sunbonnet, as it persisted in the twentieth century, was not an item of fashion. *Fairchild's Dictionary of Textiles* defines *fashion* as "[a] sociocultural phenomenon in which a preference is shared by a large number of people for a particular style that lasts for a relatively short period of time, and then is replaced by another style."[1] One of the key elements of fashion highlighted in this definition is its constant state of change. Fashion historian Lourdes Font's succinct definition of fashion—"luxury and novelty combined into an irresistible force"—also emphasizes that true high fashion is not even for the average consumer.[2] Fashion is set apart by its use of the finest and rarest materials and the most sophisticated techniques.

Dress, on the other hand, can be thought of simply as the clothes people wear. Dress may not change dramatically over the decades, or even the centuries in some cases. An article of clothing that is found to be useful and practical may continue to be used for many years as an item of working dress and may be far removed from the direction of high fashion.

Although the sunbonnet can best be thought of as a working dress garment, it is related in form and function to several types of fashionable headgear that were worn by women of various social standing and economic status in the eighteenth and nineteenth centuries. These related forms include the calash, fashionable bonnets such as the poke bonnet, and some varieties of cap, such as the mobcap.

Some commentators have attempted to trace the evolution of the sunbonnet from a single original source, such as the mobcap.[3] Even within the lofty realm of haute couture, where designers register each season's original designs with the Chambre Syndicale, there is often debate as to which designer was "the first" to change to a new silhouette, bring forth an innovation, or discard a previous convention. When looking at the working dress of previous centuries, we are left with so few reliable forms of primary evidence that to try to reconstruct the precise evolutionary trail of the sunbonnet seems speculative at best. Instead, in this section I will give an overview of a range of fashionable millinery options, all of which I believe had some influence on sunbonnet design at various points in time, without proclaiming any single one as the "true" progenitor of the sunbonnet.

The calash, or bashful bonnet, relates to the sunbonnet in both its basic shape and its function as a barrier against the elements. An eighteenth-century lavender calash from the collection of the Costume Institute (Plate 1) exemplifies this type of head covering. Like the sunbonnet, the calash was a type of protective headgear worn outside and was originally fashionable in the 1770s and 1780s. The calash was usually constructed of a plain silk, silk taffeta, or cotton fabric that was drawn over half-hoops of whalebone or cane. This headdress was collapsible when not in use, but could be drawn up over the wearer's face again by means of a cord, leading to the phrase "bashful bonnet."[4]

The calash took its name from its resemblance to a type of carriage called *calèche*, which featured a collapsible top, rather like the covering of today's convertible sports car.[5] The calash bonnet was spacious enough to accommodate the toweringly large hairstyles of the late eighteenth century, but in some places it persisted even after these hairdos had become passé. For example, the calash apparently survived into the 1830s in isolated areas of England, and in novelist Elizabeth Gaskell's *Cranford*, set during this decade but written twenty years later, she uses her characters' calashes to convey how behind the times their clothing is. Gaskell's narrator asks her 1850s reader with gentle irony, "Do you know what a calash is? It is a covering worn over caps, not unlike the heads fastened on old-fashioned gigs; but sometimes it is not quite so large."[6]

The calash was known and widely worn in the United States in the eighteenth century.[7] A sunbonnet in the collection of the Costume Institute at the Metropolitan Museum of Art utilizes a shirred construction similar to that of the calash (Plate 2). Capote bonnets in the Texas Fashion Collection (Plate 3) and the Costume Institute (Plate 4) have the shape of a modified calash, utilizing a hooped frame, but also have a quilted construction that resembles a sunbonnet with very thick padding in the brim. These bonnets may indicate that useful construction techniques were transferred between different types of headgear.

Diana de Marly argues that the British sunbonnet style called the "ugly" (one wonders whether the name was a commentary on the bonnet design or the wearer suitable for such covering), which was worn by some farm laboring women into the early twentieth century, was directly descended from the fashionable calash.[8] However, David Hackett Fischer notes the use of the term ugly to refer to a style of woman's bonnet dating to at least 1639 in the lowlands of Scotland: "A boungrace was a cloth shade or curtain attached to the front of a woman's bonnet. It was also worn in the northern counties of England, and called an 'Ugly' in Northumberland."[9] Fischer's arguments connect proto-sunbonnet styles to folk dress, worn out of tradition rather than high fashion. Fischer's theories will be discussed again in the context of nineteenth-century sunbonnets; I present these two viewpoints to highlight the difficulty in authoritatively declaring any one garment to be the predecessor of, or inspiration for, the sunbonnet.

Another form of eighteenth-century headgear related to the sunbonnet in form, although not in function, is the mobcap. Caps, unlike sunbonnets, were headcoverings worn primarily for customary rather than practical reasons: adult women of the eighteenth century were expected to cover their heads by wearing a cap at all times, unless in formal attire.[10] Caps were fashionable into the mid-nineteenth century, when they began to be supplanted by nets or snoods.[11] One style of eighteenth-century cap, the mobcap, has a gathered crown and a ruffle around the edge that is similar in structure to some later sunbonnets with crenellated crowns and a brim that is little more than a ruffle.[12] Hilda Amphlett writes that "[m]ob caps varied slightly in form but all were drawn up with a tape where the brim and crown met and so could be laid flat for laundering and ironing. All were starched."[13] These design and care elements are similar to some poke-style sunbonnet designs, which could also be unfastened for ease of ironing, and required starching to achieve the desired look and sun-protective function (see "The Poke Sunbonnet Brim" in Chapter 4).

For much of the nineteenth century, bonnets formed a key part of a fashionable woman's wardrobe. Bonnets were the essential millinery for day wear and social calls and were worn by women of all socioeconomic classes.[14] Fashionable bonnets were made of beaver, felted wool, silk velvet and plush, and leghorn and chip straw.[15] Georgine de Courtais writes, "The bonnet was the most characteristic form of feminine headwear in the 19th century and during the early Victorian period was not merely popular but was considered to be the only correct form of outdoor headcovering, except for the most informal occasions."[16] The absolute popularity of bonnets as a fashionable form of headgear in the 1800s probably influenced working women during this period to choose the sunbonnet over other forms of head covering for work wear.

The nineteenth-century ideal of the beautiful female body placed a premium on soft white skin. Bonnets played a key role in protecting a fair complexion and were augmented with veils and even calash-like visors called "uglies" (the same terminology that was used for working dress bonnets).[17]

As early as the late eighteenth century, the poke bonnet was in fashion and was the predecessor of other fashionable bonnet styles to come in the nineteenth century.[18] Some high-quality poke bonnets were made of Leghorn straw, imported from Leghorn (now Livorno) in Tuscany. The poke bonnet "evolved as a result of the influence of classicism on all aspects of dress . . . [and] emulated an idealistic if rather inaccurate notion of the classical profile."[19]

Roman women's hairstyles of the Flavian era (A.D. 69–96) featured high curls in the front with a coiled bun in the back and inspired fashionable Neoclassical hairstyles in the late eighteenth century.[20] The Flavian silhouette is also roughly analogous to that of poke bonnets from the late eighteenth and early nineteenth centuries. The poke bonnet shape would continue to dominate both fashionable bonnet and sunbonnet styles through the first half of the nineteenth century.[21]

During the Romantic period, bonnets grew larger to balance the ballooning gigot sleeves of women's dresses.[22] By the second half of the 1830s, some fashionable bonnets had developed a bavolet neck covering.[23] Some bonnets were still made of Leghorn straw and could be purchased from milliners trimmed, or untrimmed if the lady preferred to trim it herself with ribbons at home.[24] Other bonnets, similar in appearance to straw bonnets, even substituted embossed paper as the primary material.[25]

A tan and blue braided straw poke bonnet of the 1830s from the Texas Fashion Collection (Plate 5) has a four-and-one-half-inch long fabric bavolet as well as silk taffeta chin ties. The brim rises like the high curls of a Flavian-era hairstyle; the crown echoes the Roman woman's bun of coiled hair. Although this fashionable bonnet uses mixed materials, the components of the bonnet, including ties and bavolet, relate exactly to the configuration of a typical sunbonnet.

Fig. 2. Benjamin Henry Latrobe, *Nondescripts Attracted by a Neighboring Barbecue, near the Oaks, Virginia*. Pencil and ink wash, 6¹⁵⁄₁₆ x 10¹⁵⁄₁₆ in. Virginia, 1796.
Papers of Benjamin Henry Latrobe,
Maryland Historical Society, Baltimore.
Courtesy of the Maryland Historical Society.

This is interesting, as the Maryland architect Benjamin Henry Latrobe's sketch *Nondescripts Attracted by a Neighboring Barbecue, near the Oaks,Virginia,* a pencil and ink wash created in 1796, shows a sunbonnet that already possesses a distinct tail to shade the wearer's neck, well before the 1830s (Fig. 2).This evidence makes it seem less likely that developments in sunbonnets were the result of a "trickle-down" theory of fashion, in which French fashions were directly appropriated and approximated in less expensive materials. Rather, sunbonnets and fashionable bonnets seem to have run on mostly parallel but occasionally intersecting courses, with fashionable bonnets influencing sunbonnets until hats began to replace bonnets as fashionable items in the mid-nineteenth century

The 1840s saw the popularity of the bibi, or cottage, bonnet, characterized by a continuous line from crown to brim.[26] Drawn bonnets were fashionable formal bonnets during this period and, like the calash, were shirred over cords of whalebone or cane.[27] Some bonnets of this decade were trimmed with feathers, which could be dyed to match the fabric of the bonnet.[28]

From 1860 to 1865, spoon bonnets were worn, with a large gap between the head and the bonnet brim and flowers filling in this space.[29] Fashionable bonnets began to grow shorter in the back, and the bavolet began to disappear from the neck.[30] From 1865 to 1868, bonnets shrank to yet smaller and smaller sizes. By the end of the decade, fashionable unmarried women only wore bonnets for formal yet modest occasions, such as church atten-dance.[31] Hats replaced bonnets as fashionable headgear in the sec-ond half of the nineteenth century, and "the bonnet gradually took on the role of the 'proper' choice in headgear. It was particularly important for the nice-minded woman to wear a bonnet to church."[32] This idea of the dressy bonnet for church would survive into the twentieth century in rural Texas.[33]

The Nineteenth-Century Sunbonnet

In the eighteenth century, many Americans viewed country or frontier living as a respectable means to the important goal of individual land ownership. This view was not just held by individuals but was also supported by the official land divestment policy of the United States government, which gave away the bulk of public land across the country to those willing to homestead it. "The ideal was a country of free citizens, small-holders living on their own bits of land."[1] Eighteenth-century American farmers were often depicted in periodicals as independent, God-fearing, honest, and productive.[2]

Some of this pro-rural feeling remained into the nineteenth century. A women's column in the New England farm journal *Amer-*

ican *Agriculturist* argued in the 1850s, "[W]hat a relief it is to be where one may go out in morning dress and sunbonnet—may move with freedom, and breathe with no fear of contamination."[3] Country life was held up as a healthy alternative to the impurities, both moral and physical, viewed as inherent in the city of the industrial age. However, the historian Arthur Meier Schlesinger writes that by the late nineteenth century, "It was the city rather than the unpeopled wilderness that was beginning to dazzle the imagination of the nation. The farmer, once the pride of America, was descending from his lofty estate, too readily accepting the city's scornful estimate of him as a 'rube' and a 'hayseed.'"[4]

As the Hamiltonian vision of America as urban, industrial, and capitalist overwhelmed the Jeffersonian ideal of America as a nation of independent farmers, changes also occurred in the perception of accessories worn for farm work. Jules David Prown writes that in material culture analysis "[t]he underlying premise is that human-made objects reflect, consciously or unconsciously, directly or indirectly, the beliefs of the individuals who commissioned, fabricated, purchased, or used them and, by extension, the beliefs of the larger society to which these individuals belonged."[5] A seemingly simple object like a sunbonnet, therefore, has much to tell us about the person who made and wore it, as well as the society in which she lived. Prown goes on to assert that using human-made objects to reveal a society's beliefs, "when a society undergoes a traumatic change, that change should manifest itself artifactually."[6] This was true in the history of the sunbonnet; as American society became more urban during the nineteenth century, the sunbonnet declined in use. Over the course of the nineteenth century, farmers were increasingly perceived as coarse, rustic, uneducated, and unintelligent, and physical labor was considered degrading.[7] Sunbonnets, which had in the early years of the United States been imbued with positive associations of independence, would slowly come to be associated with practicality at best, and poverty and backwardness at worst, in more populated regions of the United States.

Negative associations with sunbonnets, at least among the privileged, were already creeping in by the late eighteenth century in East Coast establishment areas such as Virginia. Benjamin Henry Latrobe's sketch *Nondescripts Attracted by a Neighboring Barbecue...* characterizes late eighteenth-century sunbonnet wearers as "nondescripts," the uninteresting rural poor (see Fig. 2). However, one element leaps out as especially interesting to a viewer today regarding this rag-tag, barefoot group of mother and three children: one of the children is wearing trousers! In this 1796 sunbonnet depiction, one of the sunbonnet wearers is probably a little boy. In the eighteenth century, small children of both genders wore dresses, and only when a boy had reached a certain age (between two and eight years old, depending on the time and community) was he "breeched" and put into breeches or trousers for the first time.[8] A boy of an age to wear trousers had put aside some of the trappings of a childhood ruled by the feminine sphere, but apparently this change of dress did not mean foregoing the sunbonnet. This is the only example I have encountered of a male sunbonnet wearer older than a baby still in dresses and wearing a baby bonnet.

In the ever-westward-moving frontier areas and some rural regions, where most settlers were pursuing the dream of independent land ownership, country life and agricultural work did not become tainted with negative associations as early as they did in more eastern and urban parts of the country. In these areas, sunbonnets remained common elements of women's working dress.

In *Albion's Seed: Four British Folkways in America*, David Hackett Fischer's project is to connect the folkways of four different regions of the United States to practices already present in Britain and brought over to the New World by four distinct waves of immigration. He connects the British folk dress of the immigrant group commonly known as the Scotch-Irish (or "borderers," as Fischer terms them—a group actually composed of primarily Protestant individuals from "the north of Ireland, the lowlands of Scotland, and the northern counties of England"[9]) to clothing worn in the southern highlands and southwestern frontier of the United States.

According to Fischer, "strong continuities linked the costume of North Britain in the seventeenth century to backcountry dress ways in the eighteenth century, frontier fashions in the nineteenth century, and 'country western' clothing today."[10]

The Scotch-Irish migration pattern can be broadly summarized as the following: "From England to Scotland, from Scotland to Ireland, from Ireland to Pennsylvania, from Pennsylvania to Carolina, from Carolina to the Mississippi Valley, from the Mississippi to Texas, from Texas to California."[11] As a people, they chased the southwestern frontier farther and farther west, carrying their sunbonnets with them. The author's own ancestors participated in this pattern as far as East Texas, and most of the ancestors of the sunbonnet narrators interviewed for this book were a part of this same settlement story.

Historical evidence shows that sunbonnets were still considered valued accessories in 1830s Revolutionary Texas, rather than badges of unbecoming labor. As a preteen girl, Dilue Rose Harris was an early Anglo settler of Texas, and she later wrote a memoir describing her experiences in the Revolution. Harris recounts how she lost her sunbonnet into the alligator-infested waters of the Trinity Bay during the Runaway Scrape, while her family was making a crossing. A large alligator had killed a man there just a few days before, so no one dared to swim out to recover the sunbonnet.[12] As a result, Harris had to wear a tablecloth tied on her head for the next few days (it would have been unthinkable to go around bareheaded), which embarrassed the eleven-year-old to such an extent that she then avoided seeing any young men she knew.[13] Returning home after the Battle of San Jacinto, Harris found her older sunbonnet in a chest that had been hidden before the family fled. Harris writes, "I was prouder of that old bonnet than in after years a new white lace one that my husband gave me."[14] The sunbonnet was one of Harris's prized possessions, an accessory of treasured femininity even in the midst of the dangerous life on the Texas frontier in wartime.

Chapters nine and ten of *Adventures of Huckleberry Finn* are another useful source of nineteenth-century sunbonnet imagery. When Huckleberry and Jim locate a stash of clothing in a flood-destroyed house floating down the Mississippi River, the characters decide to take along the "two old dirty calico dresses, and a sunbonnet," as well as some other items of clothing that are hanging on the wall.[15] This short description first helps to set the time and place of the novel; the combination of calico dress and sunbonnet is strongly associated with the frontier woman.[16] This also demonstrates that textile objects were valuable possessions, not to be left to ruin even if not for the correct gender (especially for a clever boy who could see their potential).

The etiquette of the sunbonnet also figures into the plot of the novel when Huck disguises himself as a girl so he can gather the local gossip unrecognized.[17] By putting on the sunbonnet and a dress, and practicing feminine mannerisms, Huck tries unsuccessfully to impersonate a girl traveling through town.[18] When Huck visits a woman's home, one of the first things Huck's hostess suggests is that he remove his bonnet as he talks with her.[19] This is helpful for the study of sunbonnets because it demonstrates that sunbonnets were primarily worn outdoors, and it shows that hospitality may have dictated an offer to remove the bonnet in preparation for a stay indoors.[20]

This is perhaps different from the etiquette of nineteenth-century hat wear for formal social calls among those of higher social status: "[L]adies paying social visits would retain their hats while their hostesses could always be distinguished by the fact that she wore an indoor cap or went bareheaded."[21] A photograph probably from the 1830s shows two women sitting with a quilt, the hatless woman most likely the hostess, while the bonneted woman is probably paying a call.[22]

The sunbonnet also falls under the scrutiny of Twain's satirical eye. Huck, speaking from the perspective of a boy who disdains the fetters of conventional society, offers some insight into the physical limitations that sunbonnets impose. The long brim of the poke-style sunbonnet worn in the 1830s to 1840s hides the face of the wearer.[23] This is useful for Huckleberry's disguise, but he comments, "I put on the sun-bonnet and tied it under my chin, and then for a body to look in and see my face was like looking down a joint of stove-pipe."[24] Allowing for the exaggeration that is often a part of satire, a woman wearing a sunbonnet with a brim this long would struggle to see where she was going, and her face would be almost completely invisible to others. At least one cartoon of the 1820s confirms Huck's description and demonstrates how, several years prior to the setting of Twain's novel, fashionable poke bonnets had developed an exaggeratedly long brim. A cartoon from La Bibliothèque Nationale, Paris, shows women wearing poke bonnets with brims so long that men virtually disappear into the bonnet (when angling for a kiss?) or alternately are literally kept at a distance by the length of the bonnet brim.[25] Once Huck goes back on the river, he says, "I took off the sun-bonnet, for I didn't want no blinders on, then."[26] This statement emphasizes again that a woman wearing a sunbonnet is as restricted in her vision as a horse or mule with blinders on, her peripheral vision obliterated. It is tempting perhaps and not unwarranted to draw a comparison between the limitations of a woman's scope of vision when wearing extreme sunbonnet styles and the limited scope of opportunity that ambitious nineteenth-century women faced in the areas of career, political participation, and so forth.

Slat sunbonnets appeared around the middle of the nineteenth century and were widely worn throughout the last quarter of the century.[27] It is interesting to note that the slat sunbonnet, which represented a new development in the construction of the sunbonnet, gained popularity as other types of good quality or luxury bonnets were waning as high fashion headgear. The slat sunbonnet, as will be discussed more fully below, was easier to care for than quilted brim, fabric poke sunbonnets. This is an example of American sunbonnet construction developing to fulfill a functional need, rather than as a response to changing fashions on the other side of the Atlantic.

In 1852 one clever Alabama politician's wife used a slat sunbonnet to ingratiate herself with a rural constituency during her husband's congressional campaign. Virginia Tunstall Clay and her husband, Clement, were campaigning in a north Alabama region predominately populated by working-class whites on small family farms (most likely of the Scotch-Irish group described by Fischer), and she became aware that to their eyes her hat—a fashionable example of city millinery—must seem pretentious. The quick-thinking Clay arranged a trade with a local innkeeper's daughter, and soon Clay was seen sporting a sunbonnet on the campaign trail. Her new/used sunbonnet was a slat bonnet of "'pea-green cambric . . . lined with pink and stiffened with pasteboard slats.'"[28] By wearing this slat sunbonnet, she presented herself as "one of the people," a down-to-earth person the rural constituents could relate to, rather than a lofty city-dweller far removed from their way of life and their concerns. Her political use of the sunbonnet helped earn her husband the vote of that county, even though he ultimately lost his bid for Congress.[29]

Women of other immigrant groups, which settled areas of the Pacific and northwestern frontiers and the Great Plains, also adopted the sunbonnet. Present-day historian Elliott West describes the popular narrative of the nineteenth century's western settlement:

> Indians are subdued and imperial rivals are whipped or hoodwinked; tracks are laid to carry steam-belching locomotives into the continent's outback; precious metals are discovered and extracted; great herds of cattle are brought up on the grasslands; prairies and plains are transformed into farms. This story has been written far too narrowly. . . . [T]he leading actors have been almost all men. The reader assumes women and children were there, yet their roles are described so vaguely.[30]

West points out that women played a tremendous part in much of the manual labor involved in settling the West (particularly in the realm of farming).[31] He also notes that even while pioneers adapted to their new environment, they also brought with them already established values and traditions and the desire "to build what they considered a proper social order."[32] The sunbonnet is an object poised at the intersection of these two thoughts. It is a reaction in the material culture of the West to the reality of women's participation in outdoor manual labor. At the same time, the sunbonnet, whether worn on the trail or for work, speaks to norms of beauty (i.e., fair skin) dictated by the prevailing social order of the day. This sense of what was proper would have been reinforced in the minds of even the remotest pioneer woman through her memories of life back East or in her homeland, as well as through women's fashion magazines such as *Godey's Ladies Book*.

Willa Cather describes sunbonnet use among female pioneers of Scandinavian ancestry in her novel *O Pioneers!* In this novel, set in the 1880s, Cather uses imagery of the sunbonnet to illustrate her character Alexandra's departure from the established social order's expected gender roles. Alexandra is a strong woman, one who "ain't much like other women-folks," according to her brother, Lou.[33] Most white women on the frontier strove to maintain the fashionable ideals of beauty such as maintaining their fair complexions by scrupulously wearing sunbonnets and other accessories to shun the sun. However, Cather's Alexandra rejects her sunbonnet and by extension the ideals of beauty it represents. "She was standing lost in thought, leaning upon her pitchfork, her sunbonnet lying beside her on the ground,"[34] Cather writes, as if to indicate that Alexandra's thoughts tended to realms beyond fashion, ladylike propriety, and her own appearance. Later in the novel, Cather mentions the sunbonnet again, emphasizing the fact that

Alexandra could have excelled in the accepted forms of beauty if she so chose: "Her face is always tanned in summer, for her sunbonnet is oftener on her arm than on her head. But where her collar falls away from her neck . . . the skin is of such smoothness and whiteness as none but Swedish women ever possess; skin with the freshness of the snow itself."[35]

Nineteenth-century frontier and rural women had other options for sun protection besides the cloth sunbonnet. Shaker women wore bonnets that combined a flat plaited straw body with a bavolet of cloth at the back.[36] Wide-brimmed straw shade hats were also worn by women who worked outdoors, often on the grounds that they were cooler than the closely fitting sunbonnet, which some women argued kept out air and sound as well as providing shade.[37] These styles also offered the wearer a wider field of vision than the "blinder-like" effect of some sunbonnets. However, straw hats from overseas were expensive in America because of the cost of materials and import duties.[38] This made the imported straw hat an impractical extravagance for most farm women, who needed to save their pennies.

Hats woven from palm fronds were an alternative to the fine straw hat.[39] Some farm women of the northeast supplemented their incomes by making palm hats as a cottage industry.[40] Palm leaves could be relatively inexpensively imported from Cuba, and women could also weave their own hats at home.[41] Hats woven from the leaves of palm trees native to certain warmer-climate regions of the Deep South were also available. Palmetto hats were widely worn in the South due to 1860s wartime shortages. The leaves were first boiled, then sun-bleached, before being braided and sewn into hat form.[42]

However, the enduring image of the frontier or rural American woman of the 1800s is that of the woman in a sunbonnet. Unlike a straw hat, the sunbonnet was extremely inexpensive and could be made at home, rather than purchased ready-made. Unlike the palm frond hat, which required special materials and weaving skills, the sunbonnet could be quickly made from any available humble textiles by anyone with basic sewing skills. And, as an early twentieth-century publication noted, the fabric sunbonnet could withstand much more wear and tear than a straw hat: "[W]hen it is considered that such bonnets . . . will last three or more seasons if they receive any degree of care, ordinary straw hats hardly come in for comparison."[43]

By the late nineteenth century it was not even necessary for a woman to have pattern-making skills in order to make her own sunbonnet. As early as the 1880s, commercial pattern companies such as Butterick had offered sunbonnet patterns for sale. For example, the Butterick's 1882 summer catalogue included pattern

7063, a "Misses Sun-Bonnet" in one size for the price of ten cents (approximately $12.29 in 2004 U.S. dollars).[44] This pattern was for a poke-style sunbonnet and featured a generous (probably to the shoulders) tail and ruffled or ruched trim along the edge of the brim and tail.[45]

It is likely that the sunbonnet's popularity in the nineteenth century stemmed in large part from practical considerations. Cost and availability of materials, as well as ease and speed of construction, are factors that continued to weigh in favor of the sunbonnet into the twentieth century.

Twentieth-Century Transition

The folklorist Janet K. Jeffery writes, "Once the frontier closed, the sunbonnet remained in rural pockets, especially throughout the South."[1] At the end of the nineteenth century, in places where agriculture remained central to the economy, the sunbonnet survived as an essential article of women's dress, a ghost of fashion past flittering about the cotton fields. Linda Baumgarten, curator of costumes and textiles at Colonial Williamsburg, uses the phrase "fossilized fashion" to describe a similar phenomenon occurring in the areas of formal wear or ceremonial clothing, such as court dress: "deliberate retention of old-fashioned design elements for symbolic reasons."[2] She notes that preserving elements of older fashions could in some contexts imply "conservatism, dignity, and formality."[3]

However, in the case of the sunbonnet, the fossilization that occurred was due not to symbolic concerns but to more mundane reasons: put simply, it worked. Sunbonnets were very successful at keeping sunlight off the wearer's face, so for women with this goal, the sunbonnet remained a reasonable choice. The twentieth-century sunbonnet was not fashionable; it was functional. Sunbonnets had passed from any trace of parallel in fashion to become simply regional working dress.

There is one interesting exception to this statement that should be noted before proceeding into a more in-depth look at twentieth-century sunbonnets as working dress. Around the turn of the twentieth century, as women of leisure began taking up more sports activities, female golfers initiated a fad for wearing sunbonnets on the green. A simple item of dress had briefly become a sports-driven fashion.

The New York Times reported in 1903, "It was suddenly discovered that, made in pretty, becoming colors, and if not of exaggerated size, the bonnets might be becoming, and many were ordered."[4] By the turn of the twentieth century, in metropolitan areas of the Northeast such as New York City, sunbonnets had already been passé for so long that they could be reinvented as a trend. Fashion commentators were quick to distinguish these new faddish sunbonnets from their nineteenth-century counterparts:

> "Ugliness and the old-time sunbonnet were synonymous terms . . . [The fashionable new sunbonnets] are shorter in the front than the old-time bonnet, and the cape in the back is a tiny affair, useful to protect the back of the neck, but not large enough to keep out the breezes. One may both hear and see in the modern bonnet, which is not possible with the old."[5]

These fashionable sunbonnets were worn in varying solid colors, including pink, blue, red, black, or white, as well as stripes. The *Times* reported that old-fashioned gingham bonnets, in neutral colors such as brown and white, were available ready-to-wear for as little as 25 cents (which would have been a significant sum in other parts of the country); however, these were not in style. Solid white bonnets with quality lace and ruffle trimmings could cost a dollar or more; solid white was considered a wise choice. "If she is particular about having things match, she will have a white sunbonnet, which will go with everything."[6]

The fleeting fashion for sunbonnets did not hold the attention of tastemakers for long. Soon women in rural areas (who probably never even heard that sunbonnets had temporarily been fashionable) were left to carry on the sunbonnet tradition.

The East Texas women I interviewed in 2004 were among the nontrendy wearers of the sunbonnet. The observations and anecdotes these oral history narrators shared with me shed considerable light on what I have found through other sources, including other oral histories. In their own words, they told their stories and their experiences of wearing the sunbonnet, primarily as agricultural laborers working in the cotton fields. Even as cotton became less important to the East Texas economy, some of these women continued wearing sunbonnets into the later decades of the twentieth century and beyond.

From the reminiscences of my sunbonnet narrators, it seems that in many East Texas agricultural laboring families of the early 1920s and 1930s, sewing was a task often delegated to a single member of the family. Other family members were needed to work in the fields, while one person was trained to sew for the whole family.

In Minnie Lee's family, she herself was the seamstress, while her mother never learned to sew. Minnie Lee probably learned her sewing skills from her aunts.[7] Louise, whose mother died when she was three, remembers that her sister Leila did the sewing for the entire family, including sunbonnet making for the girls. This sister made her own patterns, cutting them from old newspaper.[8] Paper was too valuable to be thrown away, and any available paper could be recycled into patterns. Eileen, a woman who now sells sunbonnets at the Nacogdoches Trade Days in Nacogdoches, Texas, received her first sunbonnet pattern from her mother, who was adept at cutting her own patterns. This particular pattern had been cut out from a monthly free newspaper about farming.[9]

In the early twentieth century, home-drawn patterns for sunbonnets were passed from neighbor to neighbor. Although, as previously noted, commercial patterns had been available since the nineteenth century, purchased patterns were not common among sewers in East Texas.[10] A woman who admired her friend's sunbonnet would ask for the pattern, just as one might ask for a friend's recipe.[11] *Loblolly* narrator Mrs. Ruby Youngblood used a pattern that had been in her family for as long as she could remember, about eighty years.[12] Similarly, in Arkansas, one family reports passing down a sunbonnet pattern through four generations of twentieth-century women (although the third and fourth generations did not wear the sunbonnet for work purposes).[13] If a woman did not have a pattern, she might simply pull apart an old, worn-out sunbonnet to use as a cutting guide.[14]

Although a seamstress could sew a sunbonnet "on her fingers" (by hand), by the early twentieth century most sunbonnets were sewn on a treadle sewing machine.[15] Eileen still uses her 1945 Singer treadle sewing machine. She never learned how to use an electric sewing machine but believes that some of the work would be harder to do on an electric machine, such as turning corners on the quilted brim of a poke-style sunbonnet.[16] In my own sewing experience, as a person who learned to sew on a foot-powered machine before venturing into the speedy world of electricity, I have to agree—I stop and turn the wheel manually on my electric machine when turning precise corners.

Mrs. Ruby Youngblood says that she can sew a sunbonnet in about five minutes after cutting the pieces. She describes the sunbonnet-making process this way:

> I always cut the brim and the ruffle, then the crown with the tail on it. You'd sew the ruffle to the brim, which has a lining on the inside. After hemming the tail, you would sew a thin strip 'cross the neck and run a little string of material through it. A little hole is cut in the middle and drawn up as tight as you like. Then tie [it] in a knot. Sew the brim and crown together. Then stitch your ties on at the base of your brim and crown.[17]

Eileen finds that as she has gotten older, it now takes her about two hours, start to finish, to construct a sunbonnet; when she was younger, the process took about half that time.[18]

The folklorist Janet K. Jeffery, writing in the early 1990s, notes that "[t]he frugal life on the frontier dictated bonnet materials. Fabric had to be durable, easily obtained, and affordable."[19] Nineteenth-century sunbonnets were made from a variety of fabrics, including "[c]alico, coarse muslin (both solid and printed), checkered gingham, chambray" for everyday bonnets, and "sateen, fine sheer wool crepe, wool rep, silk taffeta, and even curtain scrim" for dress bonnets.[20]

The principles of durability, availability, and affordability continued to hold true for twentieth-century sunbonnet makers as well. Sunbonnets of the early twentieth century were made from a variety of fabric designs, including solids and gingham checks.[21] Mrs. Ruby Youngblood made sunbonnets from "any kind of prints that are thick enough, 'Dan River' or gingham, any kind of design is all right."[22] Dan River refers to the type of cotton calico apparel fabrics once manufactured by the Dan River Inc. textile company (in 2008 a supplier of home products as well as fabrics).

The type of material chosen for a sunbonnet provided clues as to the wearer's age and reflected the social norms of the community. Faye remembered that in the 1920s and 1930s etiquette dictated the proper fabrics for sunbonnets at different times of the year. Women wore "dark colors for winter, light colors for summer," while children would always wear lighter colors, such as floral prints and gingham.[23] It was also essential that a work bonnet be made of a washable fabric, usually cotton.[24]

The prosperity of a family determined whether a sunbonnet was made of new or used fabrics. Minnie Lee's family made their sunbonnets from new fabric scraps left over from the construction of dresses.[25] Similarly, Faye recalled that in the 1920s and

1930s her family would make trips to town (Nacogdoches, Texas) to pick fabric for a new outfit: "[Y]ou'd usually have a dress and a bonnet, matching."[26] More budget-constrained families might recycle previously used fabric into sunbonnets; for example, a faded and worn dress might find new life as a sunbonnet.

For East Texans living in company-owned sawmill towns, their options for purchasing fabric were dictated by the company, not the open market. Sawmill workers were paid in coin-shaped company chits, which were redeemable at the company-owned commissary. The commissary was the primary source of new fabrics for their sunbonnets.[27]

Printed cotton feed or flour sacks were once a source of fabric for early twentieth-century sunbonnet sewers.[28] The availability of this inexpensive material largely eliminated the need for budgeting families to weave fabric at home.[29] Faye was careful to emphasize that she did not have to wear the feed or flour sack material, which must have carried a stigma, despite its prevalence:

> People utilized everything they had. I can remember, I didn't have to have it, but during the Depression, people would make things out of food or flour sacks—it was just a print, like a bolt of material. Kids would come to school wearing it, and I'd recognize the flour sacks. And I knew they were, because we had bought the same flour! We never did wear the flour sack dresses.[30]

Louise remembered that in the early twentieth century field sun-bonnets in her family were usually made from recycled materials: "The ones we worked in were made out of old clothes. We didn't go buy new material for that. We just used what we had, you know. So old clothes of any kind."[31] Textiles were a valuable commodity for agricultural workers of the early twentieth century; a fabric would be reused multiple times until it "wore out."

This thrifty use and reuse meant that many sunbonnets of the early twentieth century did not survive; they were worn until they fell apart. Museum fashion collections tend to be weighted toward formal and ceremonial fashion and have fewer items of working dress in general for this reason. At the same time, most of the sun-bonnets that are still preserved also owe their continued existence to East Texans' prudence with textile possessions. Faye noted that she saved one of her grandmother's everyday bonnets for many years: "I quit wearing it, but I kept it all these years. I kept it, though it had gone out of style; it was still serviceable."[32] For many women in the last generation of sunbonnet wearers, whose attitudes toward possessions and finances were shaped by the Great Depression, it was and is unthinkable to throw away or give away an object that might yet prove to be useful.

Components of the Sunbonnet

The sunbonnet generally contains the basic components of brim, crown, ties, and tail.[1] Previous writers have usually classified sunbonnets as either poke-style or slat based on the construction and support method of the brim. The term *poke-style sunbonnet* evokes the long, pointed (or "poking") brims of the late eighteenth century and early nineteenth century.[2] In its current usage, *poke-style* refers to any sunbonnet that is not a slat bonnet, whether that bonnet relies on quilting, shirring, or simply multiple layers of starched fabric to reinforce the brim; these sunbonnets also usually require starch for additional brim stiffness.

Sunbonnets also come in a wide variety of silhouettes, which to some extent cross construction methods. The silhouette of a

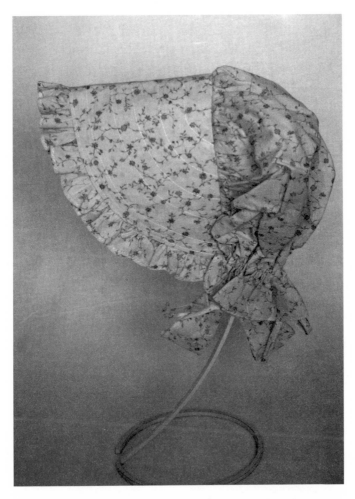

Fig. 3. Lavender poke-style sunbonnet. 1980s, East
Texas. Private collection.

Photograph by the author.

sunbonnet is determined by the depth and angle of the brim as it surrounds the wearer's face, which involves a balance between sun protection and maintaining the wearer's field of vision. Eileen prefers to make a small brim style that allows the wearer to see out with ease.[3] As Janet K. Jeffery notes, "Some brims begin at the back of the head and extend 12 inches to the front, reducing the crown to a minimum. Others begin halfway forward on the head and extend seven or eight inches over the eyes."[4] The basic silhouettes for sunbonnet brims include square, rounded, and bill-shaped brims.

Square silhouette brims end in a right angle either around the wearer's jawline or below. This silhouette is the most protective but also the most limiting in terms of the wearer's vision and air circulation. As one 1916 publication providing patterns for poke-style sunbonnets stated, "If the head-piece [brim] of a sunbonnet is square, the ruffles at the sides act as blinders, and thus cause the wearer much discomfort."[5] Slat sunbonnets very often have a square silhouette, but this silhouette may also be found in poke-style or quilted brim sunbonnets. For example, compare a yellow calico slat bonnet from the author's collection (Plate 6) with a poke-style sunbonnet that belonged to Lelia Rusk (Plate 7).[6]

Rounded silhouette sunbonnets curve over the wearer's cheek and often have quilting lines or other design elements to emphasize the curve. Slat bonnets more rarely have this silhouette, as it requires rounding the edges of the staves and casings. For example, compare a twentieth-century daisy print poke-style sunbonnet in a private collection (Plate 8) with a nineteenth-century slat bonnet from the Costume Institute (Plate 9). The Ruby Duke sunbonnet (Plate 10) shows yet another variation on the rounded silhouette.[7]

The third silhouette, the bill-shaped brim, is usually seen in a poke-style sunbonnet and could be thought of as a subset of the rounded silhouette. However, contrast the gently curving brim of the Ruby Duke sunbonnet with a blue, printed "gingham" sunbonnet (the checks in the design are printed on the surface rather than created by the weave pattern of the textile, as in a true gingham) in the author's collection (Plate 11). The bill-shaped silhouette has a brim that is significantly longer over the top of the head and slants away sharply on the sides.

The Poke Sunbonnet Brim

For the poke-style sunbonnet, the brim must be stiffened in order to achieve a shape that will stand away from the face. Poke-style sunbonnet brims are usually stiffened through quilting.[8] These brims have a thickness composed of multiple layers, which are held together by a quilting stitch. In the nineteenth century, the quilted brim of a sunbonnet often combined multiple fabric lay-

Fig. 4. Some Hispanic women wore slat sunbonnets for
agricultural work in South Texas. Russell Lee, "Mexican girl
bunching carrots, near Edinburg, Texas," February 1939,
Library of Congress, Prints and Photographs Division, FSA-OWI Collection,
LC-USF33-011976-M4 DLC
(b&w film nitrate neg.).

Fig. 5. A crenellated crown sunbonnet worn by Lizzie
Duff, a resident of Wisdom, Kentucky, in 1954.
"Roadside Holiday, U.S.A." *Vogue*
(March 1, 1954), 152.
Moser/*Vogue*, © Condé Nast Publications.

ers with a layer of crinoline (horsehair). [9] For example, one sunbonnet from the Museum of Texas Tech University (Plate 12) uses this technique. Most twentieth-century sunbonnets simply have an extra layer (or layers) of fabric quilted in between the inner and outer brim; this extra layer was usually starched prior to insertion. [10]

The extra fabric in the poke-style brim could have been recycled from old clothes, even if new material was used for the exterior of the sunbonnet. In fact, one sewing instruction booklet from 1916 urged its students,

> The best material for this purpose is that obtained from the skirt part of an old nainsook night dress or from the back of a man's shirt that is worn past mending. . . . Material of this kind is best for the reason that it has been washed so many times that all the stiffening has been removed and it is therefore soft enough to absorb starch; then, too, its softness permits it to be quilted through more evenly than would be the case with new material. [11]

Some quilted brim sunbonnets were made with a batting layer of cotton from the family's own fields. [12] Through a process called carding, cotton can be hand cleaned of trash and seeds. This process also smooths and aligns the fibers. In the carding process, a pair of wooden bats, called cards, with wire needles on the inside were used to prepare the cotton fiber for use as batting.[13] Not all families possessed a set of cards, but if they did, they would be able to use their own cotton resources to line the brims of their sunbonnets.[14] The drawback to using carded cotton batting in sunbonnet brims was that care was necessary in washing, or the cotton would pack down or knot in areas of the brim.[15] This type of cotton batting was used in a child's sunbonnet from the Museum of Texas Tech University (Plate 13), which has a brim hand-quilted in parallelogram shapes (Plate 14). In areas of loss on the bonnet brim, the cotton batting is visible. Cotton batting can also be seen through areas of loss on an entirely quilted silk sunbonnet from the Texas Fashion Collection (Plates 15 and 16).

Poke-style sunbonnet brims were quilted in a variety of patterns. It was in the design of the quilting stitches that sunbonnet makers were most dramatically able to add an element of individual self-expression to an otherwise utilitarian object. Quilting on a sunbonnet brim may appear in straightforward lines or may take on a variety of ornamental shapes, including curves, diamonds, squares, hexagons, or lozenges.[16] Lines of quilting may either run in a straight path across the brim or follow the cut of the lower brim edge in an L shape or curve.

The more ornate quilting patterns, along with the fabric used, distinguished better quality sunbonnets.[17] One sunbonnet from the Museum of Texas Tech University has a brim that is quilted in one-and-one-half-inch mazelike spiraling squares (Plate 12). Louise remembers some sunbonnets were quilted like "old-timey rail fence rows. You know, zigzag-like across the brim."[18] A black silk dress bonnet in the Texas Fashion Collection (Plate 17) has a machine-quilted crossing zigzag pattern, as well as lines of straight quilting parallel with the brim. Ruby Duke's sharply curving, bill-shaped sunbonnet brim (Plate 10) is quilted in patterns of interlocking circles, while Lelia Rusk's square brim sunbonnet (Plate 7) is complemented by square quilting. Faye's mother quilted in much more elaborate patterns, such as stars, or would even trace a shape from a catalog or paper, a doll for instance, and quilt that shape onto the sunbonnet brim.[19]

Other materials occasionally were used for additional brim stiffening. A black silk sunbonnet from the Museum of Texas Tech University (Plate 18) has a brim that is hand-quilted in parallelogram shapes and stiffened with cotton batting, but also has a wire support along the outer brim edge. In the twentieth century, in some regions, straw matting was available in stores for use in poke-style sunbonnet brims.[20] In addition to the fact that such matting had to be purchased, as opposed to the more cost-effective recycling of old fabrics, a sunbonnet on a foundation of straw could not be laundered and was therefore much less practical in the heat

Fig. 6. A sunbonnet that resembles the mobcap. Arthur
Rothstein, "Mrs. Bailey Nicholson, Shenandoah National
Park, Virginia," October 1935,
*Library of Congress, Prints and Photographs Division,
FSA-OWI Collection, LC-USF3301-002173-M1
(b&w film dup. neg., 4x5 size).*

of Texas. None of the East Texas women I interviewed mentioned this type of sunbonnet construction.

Sunbonnet brim trims were another way in which sunbonnet creators could express their creativity. Poke sunbonnets might be trimmed with self-fabric ruffles.[21] These ruffles were often located along the outer edge of the brim, framing the wearer's face. A 1980s lilac sunbonnet in a private collection is edged in self-fabric ruffles (Fig. 3). The Ruby Duke blue gingham sunbonnet from the early twentieth century has a brim edged in self-fabric pleats (Plate 10).

Brims were also trimmed with other materials. A sunbonnet in the Texas Fashion Collection (Plate 19) has crocheted trim along the brim and edge of the crown. Another sunbonnet in the Texas Fashion Collection (Plate 17) has machine-made lace trimming the brim and the front portion of the tail. Yet another Texas Fashion Collection sunbonnet (Plate 20) is trimmed in machine-made eyelet.

For the sunbonnet maker who had the time to spend on exquisite details, finishing techniques were another way to distinguish her work from the run-of-the-mill sunbonnet. While poke-style brim ruffles could be machine-finished, adding a lace trim at the same time, the sewer more adept at hand-work might choose instead to finish her ruffle with a rolled hem or very tiny hem, and then whip-stitch on the lace trim.[22]

Poke Sunbonnet Starching

Quilted brim poke-style sunbonnets require starching to achieve the proper stiffness needed to shade the wearer's face. Flour starch could be made at home, using basic kitchen ingredients. One flour starch recipe called for two heaping tablespoons of flour plus one level tablespoon of salt. A small amount of cold water was stirred in to create a paste. Two cups of boiling water were then gradually added, "stirring continuously and cooking until the mixture has a smooth creamy texture and reaches the desired thickness."[23] The starch was then allowed to cool. A wet sunbonnet was then dipped into the mixture, drip-drained of excess starch, then hung to dry outside. Starched sunbonnets were often dried over a fence post to retain their shape. One variation on this basic recipe called for coffee rather than water, and was used for dark color fabrics; this prevented the starch residue from showing up as white on a darker ground material.[24]

Later, many women used mass-produced starch products to give their sunbonnets the correct shape. Louise used a blue box of powdered Faultless starch to starch her bonnets. She used the cold water starching method. This involves mixing a half cup powdered starch with one and a half cups cold water, then placing the bonnet to be starched into this mixture.[25] One early twentieth-century source recommends adding two or three drops of turpentine to

Fig. 7. A mobcap-like sunbonnet worn in North Carolina. Jack
Delano, "This woman and her daughter are helping their
neighbors plant their tobacco field. The bonnet is homemade.
On U.S. 15, about five miles northeast of Durham, North
Carolina," May 1940,
Library of Congress, Prints and Photographs Division, FSA-OWI Collection,
LC-USF34-040682-D DLC (b&w film neg.).

the starch mixture to prevent the starch from sticking to one's iron.[26] The bonnet is then wrung out, smoothed, and allowed to air dry. Louise often allowed her sunbonnets to dry inside, lying flat on a towel.[27] When the bonnet has dried, it is sprinkled with water and ironed. *Loblolly* narrator Mrs. Ruby Youngblood described starching: "You are supposed to have the brim real stiff using starch and ironing while wet."[28] The result is a stiff bonnet brim that will stand up off the wearer's face.[29]

Starching and ironing sunbonnets is a time-consuming and difficult process. Before the advent of electricity, some irons were hollow, to be heated with a filling of hot coals, charcoal, or heated iron slugs.[30] Another type of early iron was the sadiron, made of as much as ten pounds of solid cast iron, which was heated by placing the iron on the hearth or stove.[31] The first electric hand-held iron was patented in 1882, and by 1900 the electric iron was commercially available in many urban areas.[32] However, in the early twentieth century most rural East Texas families possessed few or no electrical appliances, and ironing usually meant using an extremely heavy sadiron. Faye remembered their family's sadiron being placed directly in the fire.[33] Mrs. Youngblood humorously describes the difficulty of starching and ironing poke-style sunbonnets: "I would rather take a whipping than to starch and iron bonnets."[34] Despite the laboriousness of the process, even everyday field sunbonnets that were of the poke style were still starched and ironed before wearing. [35]

The Slat Sunbonnet Brim

Slat sunbonnets relied on staves, usually strips of cardboard or wood, to hold the brim of the bonnet away from the wearer's face (Plate 21). The brim of the slat sunbonnet was sewn as a series of casings. Into the casing, a strip of cardboard or wood would be inserted, to give the brim the necessary stiffness. Faye's apt simile to describe the shape of the staves is "like the flat part of a fan."[36]

A nineteenth-century blue cotton sunbonnet in the collection of the Costume Institute at the Metropolitan Museum of Art (Plate 9) uses wooden slats, with the inside opening edge of the casings hand-basted closed. For this sunbonnet to be washed, its owner would have had to unpick the basting stitches and remove the staves. After laundering, the staves would be reinserted and the brim resewn. However, this construction probably kept the staves securely in place.

As early as the mid-nineteenth century, cracker and soap boxes were made into staves for sunbonnets.[37] Any type of box could be used for making cardboard staves. Minnie Lee noted that her family would use any kind of stiff paper or cardboard they could find for the staves, as paper was scarce.[38] A brown sunbonnet in the collection of the Costume Institute, dated 1850, alternates casings of cardboard staves and delicate wooden dowels in its brim (Plates 22 and 23).

Louise Rusk remembered cutting out "pasteboard staves," about one and one-half inches wide and about six to eight inches long, to slip into the brims of her slat sunbonnets in the 1930s.[39] *Loblolly* narrator Mrs. Odell Youngblood describes the slat sunbonnets her mother made as having casings two inches wide and six inches long.[40] A sunbonnet in the Texas Fashion Collection (Plate 24) has ten one-and-one-half-inch-wide by six-and-one-half-inch-long casings for its stiff pasteboard staves.

Cardboard and wood were not the only materials used for slats. Women in different regions used whatever materials were readily available to them in constructing their sunbonnets. In Arkansas, corn husks were used to stiffen sunbonnets.[41]

The stave system made slat sunbonnets easy to care for as compared to quilted-brim poke sunbonnets, which had to be heavily starched after each washing. The cardboard staves were simply removed before washing, then reinserted after the sunbonnet was dry.[42] In Louise's family, their slat sunbonnets were not ironed before wearing, making the slat sunbonnet an important labor-saver.[43]

Because the slat sunbonnet construction allowed the brim to stand so far out from the wearer's face, much more of the brim lining was visible than in the case of poke-style sunbonnets. On these bonnets, sometimes the inner brim fabric was exactly the same as the outer brim fabric, because a single piece of material had been folded in half and stitched to form the casings for the slats. In other cases, a contrasting color fabric was used on the inside of the brim. One slat sunbonnet from the collection of the Museum of Texas Tech University (Plate 25) has a windowpane check fabric on the outside of the brim and a contrasting pink lining. A Farm Security Administration (FSA) photograph from 1939 shows a Hispanic carrot worker wearing a slat bonnet that appears to have a contrasting brim lining (Fig. 4).

Slat sunbonnets were more likely to be used for fieldwork, so the brims are less often trimmed than poke-style sunbonnet brims. However, one sunbonnet from the Texas Fashion Collection (Plate 24) has a neatly tailored cuff along the outer brim edge. A slat sunbonnet might also be trimmed with rick-rack (Plate 25). A slat sunbonnet from the Costume Institute (Plate 9) even has a self-fabric ruffle along the outer and brim edge and where the brim and crown join.

The Crown

The crown of a sunbonnet often has fullness created by the way the crown is attached to the sunbonnet brim. Additional volume may be achieved through starching.[44] The crown of a poke-style sunbonnet may retain a puffiness reminiscent of women's fashionable sleeve puffs of the 1830s. Crowns on many slat sunbonnets, on the other hand, often have a flatter, less decorative shape.

The crown may be joined to the sunbonnet's brim in a variety of ways. The majority of sunbonnets have a crown that is fully connected to the brim through stitching. There may be a simple straight seam or the crown may be pleated at this seam, as is often the case in poke-style sunbonnets. Many sunbonnets have straight seams on the sides of the brim, with pleats on the top of the sunbonnet. This type of sunbonnet could be extremely labor intensive to launder, as at least in some cases women would disassemble the sunbonnet for washing, then restitch it afterward.[45]

The crown may only be connected to the brim at intervals, creating a series of decorative loops that stand out over the brim. These crenellated crowns often button or snap to the brim and can be easily disassembled for washing and ironing. The crown of a sunbonnet in the Texas Fashion Collection (Plate 19) buttons to three sides of its brim through a series of eleven off-white buttons. Another Texas Fashion Collection sunbonnet (Plate 24) has seven buttons that anchor the brim to the crown every two and one-half inches or so. (These off-white buttons are mismatched, indicating the "make-do and reuse" nature of sunbonnet construction.) The sunbonnet worn by Lizzie Duff in a 1954 *Vogue* road travel article is another example of the crenellated crown sunbonnet (Fig. 5).[46] Some twentieth-century poke-style sunbonnets from states in the upper South, such as Virginia and North Carolina, have narrow, very ruffled brims and extremely full crowns, closely resembling mobcaps of the late eighteenth century.[47] Compare the mobcap-style bonnets from Virginia (Fig. 6) and North Carolina (Fig. 7) with Kentuckian Lizzie Duff's sunbonnet (Fig. 5). The crenellated crown sunbonnet may be a further development of the earlier cap style.

A variation on the crenellated crown sunbonnet has the crown partly sewn in a flat seam to the brim and partly fastened at intervals. The crown of one sunbonnet in the Texas Fashion Collection (Plate 20) has fullness created at the lower parts of the crown through a series of three snaps on each side, attaching crown to brim.

The crown may also contain inner construction that helps create and support its shape. Some sunbonnets contain a circular inner piece of fabric that separates the brim area from the crown. This piece of fabric is drawn up by means of a nearly circular drawstring. This component may be used in slat (for example, in the sunbonnet pictured in Plate 25) or poke-style sunbonnets (for example, in the Ruby Duke sunbonnet, Plate 10). An unusual type of inner crown construction is present in a blue chambray sunbonnet from the Museum of Texas Tech University (Plate 26). In this sunbonnet, the back of the crown has a flat horseshoe shape, resembling the back view of a calash (Plate 27). Between this flat back of the crown and the brim, there is a high but narrow puff. This puff is actually created by means of a series of interior ties (Plate 28). In each set of ties, one tie is on the crown side of the sunbonnet and the other tie is connected to the brim. When these ties are brought together, the crown assumes its high, puffed shape. The crown of a sunbonnet may also be decorated with trim; usually this decorative element is continued from another part of the sunbonnet, such as the brim or the edge of the tail.

While most of the crown variations described here have evolved for aesthetic reasons, some differences in crown size are for practical reasons. Eileen states that she does not like to alter her standard sunbonnet pattern in order to make a sunbonnet with an especially full crown; however, she does occasionally make full crown sunbonnets by special request. She explains that most of these requests for larger crown sunbonnets come from Pentecostal women, who need more fullness in the crown to accommodate their hairstyles.[48] Most Pentecostal women in East Texas wear their hair long and uncut, in accordance with the denomination's interpretation of New Testament scripture. The United Pentecostal Church International describes its guidelines:

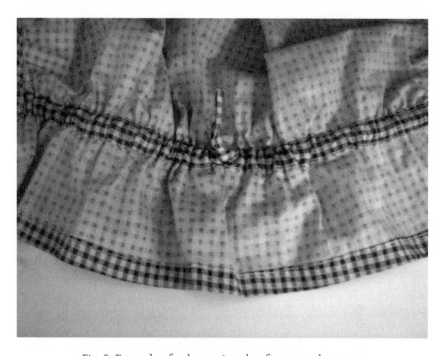

Fig. 8. Example of a drawstring that fastens at the center-
back of wearer's neck; other drawstrings may tie on one
side. Detail of sunbonnet (Plate 11) from author's collection.
Photograph by the author.

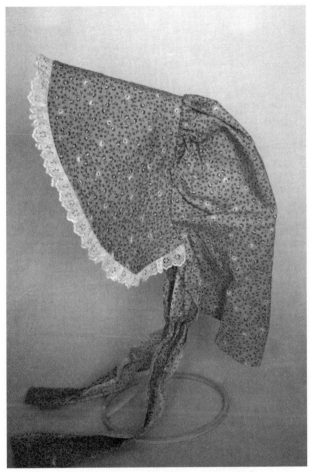

Fig. 9. This calico, poke-style sunbonnet does
not have a drawstring at the back of the
neck. 1980s, East Texas. Private collection.
Photograph by the author.

Christians can often [be] identified as such by their outward appearance. . . . Since we adhere as carefully and closely to the Scriptures as possible in matters pertaining to salvation, we also measure the standards of Christian practicalities such as clothing, by the same rule. . . . [The apostolic Christian woman's] hair style is again predicated upon the Word of God, which teaches her to let her hair grow uncut: "Is it comely that a woman pray unto God uncovered? Doth not even nature itself teach you, that, if a man have long hair, it is a shame unto him? But if a woman have long hair, it is a glory to her: for her hair is given her for a covering" (1 Corinthians 11:13–15).[49]

Many Pentecostal women wear their long hair pulled up, such as in a bun or twist, and the volume of this hair necessitates a fuller crown when they choose a sunbonnet. Thus, the size of a sunbonnet crown can even sometimes be a reflection of religious belief.

Drawstrings and Ties

Drawstrings are generally located on the inside of a sunbonnet at the back of the neck (Fig. 8). Drawstrings allow the wearer to adjust the fit of a sunbonnet. In construction, the drawstring was threaded through a casing, often using a safety pin. These drawstrings are usually made from the same fabric as the rest of the sunbonnet. Drawstrings may be left unhemmed, as they are located inside the sunbonnet and do not show.[50]

Drawstrings could also be made from other materials, such as men's shoestrings.[51]

Not all sunbonnets have drawstrings. A twentieth-century sunbonnet in a private collection has a fused crown and tail, without a drawstring at the neck (Fig. 9). In this sunbonnet, the crown flows unencumbered from a pleated seam attaching it to the brim, all the way over the wearer's neck, forming a tail that comes to just above the wearer's shoulder.

One of the typical characteristics of a sunbonnet is that it ties under the wearer's chin, to ensure a snug fit while working. The ties under the chin are usually hemmed along the edge.[52] Sometimes ties for a sunbonnet were cut out along the selvage of the fabric, utilizing every piece of the valuable textile and avoiding the need to hem the ties. Ties were sometimes pieced together from multiple fabric scraps, as in a sunbonnet from the Texas Fashion Collection (Plate 20); in this sunbonnet, the right chin tie is one piece of fabric, but the left tie is pieced together from two scraps.

Many sunbonnets have outer ties at the back of the wearer's neck, in addition to, or sometimes instead of, ties under the chin. These ties often cover the area drawn up by the inner drawstring. Some sunbonnets may rely on these ties alone to adjust the fit of the neck (Fig. 9). While the classic definition of a sunbonnet includes under-chin ties, and a sunbonnet-like garment without these ties might perhaps more accurately be characterized as a sun-hat, this book includes a broad range of headcoverings that conform to the basic sunbonnet silhouette as sunbonnets.

Dress sunbonnets sometimes used more formal materials for ties, including ribbon, as in a fashionable bonnet. A dress bonnet of black silk satin in the collection of the Costume Institute (Plate 29) has ties of grosgrain ribbon.

The placement of ties under the chin apparently offered an outlet for the wearer's nervous energy, as well; at least one person recalled little girls being scolded for chewing on their sunbonnet ties![53]

The Tail

The length of the tail was determined by the amount of neck and shoulder protection desired by the sunbonnet creator. The clothing the sunbonnet was to accompany was a factor in determining tail length, with lower necklines of a dress demanding a longer tail.[54] An unusual sunbonnet in the collection of the Museum of Texas Tech University (Plate 26) has an extralong tail, fourteen and one-half inches long, which would have swept down nearly to the wearer's elbow.[55] The tail of some sunbonnets came only to the collar and did not touch the wearer's shoulder.[56] Other sunbonnets in the early twentieth century had a tail that did come to the shoulders, to protect the wearer's entire neck.[57]

A twentieth-century lilac sunbonnet in a private collection has a tail that is simply a short ruffle, connected to the ruffles that edge the sunbonnet's brim (Fig. 3). This sunbonnet would not have made an effective sun shield; its self-ruffles along the brim coupled with the short tail suggest that this style may have originally been worn as a visiting bonnet.

Some sunbonnets are sewn with the crown and tail from separate pieces of fabric. Other sunbonnets have the crown and tail of a single length of fabric, but divided in the middle of the neck ties and inner drawstring. A sunbonnet in the Texas Fashion Collection (Plate 30) has a crown and tail of a single piece of fabric, which is only adjustable at the neck by means of outer neck ties.

Sunbonnet construction followed many different patterns, each dictated by the different desires of the wearer and the creator. But ultimately, whether of the poke style or slat variety, these sunbonnets had certain essential characteristics in common: a brim and tail for skin protection, a crown to cover the hair, and drawstrings and ties to ensure fit.

Dress Sunbonnets

In the nineteenth century and very early twentieth century, rural women had at least two sets of bonnets: "Sunday" (or "Sunday-go-to-meeting") or "visiting" sunbonnets and "everyday" sunbonnets.[1] The Sunday bonnet seems to have been a holdover from the fashionable bonnets worn to church in the nineteenth century. However, by the early twentieth century, it was becoming less common for women of East Texas and other areas of the rural South to wear a bonnet for dress occasions.[2] Fashionable hats were often worn for more formal occasions, and younger women in particular craved more contemporary forms of millinery. Older women, however, whose youth belonged to the nineteenth century, still wore dress bonnets.[3] Dress bonnets were a topic of conversation for these women "after church, at church dinners, or socials."[4]

Dress bonnets of the twentieth century were usually either black or white; black bonnets tended to be made of nonwashable fibers such as silk, while the white cotton bonnets were masterpieces in the art of laundering and starching. Dress bonnets in rural East Texas were essentially poke-style sunbonnets cut from more valuable materials than those used for everyday bonnets. A quilted brim sunbonnet in a less formal fabric than silk taffeta might have been worn by older women in the early twentieth century when "going visiting."[5]

Some Sunday bonnets were made of an all-cotton material with a silky hand, somewhat similar to a polished cotton.[6] Dress bonnets were more elaborately trimmed than the simple bonnets worn for field work. Some dress bonnets were edged with lace, tatting, or ruffles, while others might be decorated with buttons or appliqués.[7] Dress bonnets might also be decorated with embroidery stitches. Folklore columnist Pearl Lowe Boyd (1904–1965) recalled that during her childhood in Kentucky, dress bonnets for visiting the neighbors were usually white, with frills, and sometimes were even appliquéd with floral motifs.[8]

Eileen's grandmother had a white Sunday bonnet of the two-piece style, with rows of "little tiny buttons" attaching the brim to the crown. Since this bonnet served a primarily decorative function, its tail was much shorter than those of sunbonnets used for field work. The white Sunday bonnet was decorated with tatting. Eileen also remembers her mother-in-law having a dress bonnet in two pieces, which she simply "whipped together" (whip-stitched by hand) to wear. Eileen recalls that this bonnet had to be cold-water starched and had no "tail to protect the neck."[9]

Boyd noted that white visiting bonnets were not "as big or as enveloping as the darker everyday bonnet."[10] A narrower cut is a hallmark of the dress sunbonnet. These sunbonnets often are of the bill-shape silhouette and provided much less sun protection than everyday or field bonnets, which were intended to provide a full day's shade.

Faye described cotton dress bonnets with tiny ruffles and lace, which were hand pleated using starch after each washing.[11] Faye's mother and grandmother also wore black taffeta bonnets for church and going out into the community. Many of these black taffeta sunbonnets, carefully saved for best, still survive in collections, such as the Texas Fashion Collection and the Museum of Texas Tech University. Faye's grandmother also wore her dress bonnet when sitting outside on her porch in the afternoon. Faye, however, wore Sunday hats. Julia also wore small hats to church when she was young.[12] Faye also noted that hats were more fashionable than sunbonnets, and sunbonnets were worn to church by those who could not afford a store-bought hat.[13] The association of the sunbonnet with low-income status may have been one of the factors leading to its decline.

Louise remembered her Grandmother Lankford wearing a "little black taffeta bonnet" for dress occasions. This was a poke-style bonnet, with a quilted brim slightly smaller than the brims of sunbonnets worn for field work. The bonnet did not have any extra decorations, such as the ruffles placed on some dress bonnets, but the taffeta fabric made the bonnet a special occasion accessory. As young women of the 1930s, however, Louise and her sisters wore store-bought hats rather than sunbonnets for dress occasions, such as church.[14]

Pearl Lowe Boyd, writing in 1950, was struck by the contrast between mid-twentieth-century technology and the nineteenth-century look of dress sunbonnets:

> [I]n some areas I still see a little old lady in her decent black dress, fresh clean apron, and her big, black sunbonnet. . . . She may be in a fine new car with her children and her children's children dressed in the most modern styles, but, clinging to what she had known since her youth, she has an inner dignity exemplified in the sunbonnet of an era nearly past.[15]

Boyd seems to view the sunbonnet in the midcentury automobile as an honorable anachronism. I do find it interesting to note, however, that as early as 1916 a British publication suggested that a dress sunbonnet of dotted Swiss with Venetian lace trim "answers very well as an automobile bonnet."[16] When society experiences change in one realm of technology, we often look to already existing material culture forms to help us navigate this transformation; thus a motorist of 1916 prevents the windblown look created by the new mode of transport using a form of millinery known for its rigorous wind-blocking effect.

6

Context of Twentieth-Century Work Sunbonnets

The sunbonnet was ubiquitous for rural white women in East Texas in the early twentieth century. As Faye reminisced, "You didn't look different than anyone else; everyone wore them."[1] In the 1930s in East Texas, the sunbonnets chosen for field work were usually slat sunbonnets, which used staves of cardboard to hold the bonnet brim away from the face. Most women only owned one everyday sunbonnet at a time.[2]

Many women remember wearing sunbonnets while working in the cotton fields of East Texas, chopping and picking cotton by hand.[3] As a teenager, Louise wore sunbonnets as she worked on the farm her father rented. Louise's Grandmother Lankford also wore sunbonnets for working outside. Later, Louise remembers

Fig. 10. A woman in a slat sunbonnet watches as a bag of
hand-picked cotton is weighed. Dorothea Lange, "Cotton
weighing near Brownsville, Texas," August 1936,
*Library of Congress, Prints and Photographs Division, FSA-OWI
Collection, LC-USF34-009787-E (b&w film nitrate neg.).*

earning day-laborer's wages of fifty cents per hundred pounds of cotton picked. In the first half of the twentieth century, cotton was picked by hand by workers trailing long bags after them as they made their way down the row. It was then weighed (Fig. 10). One hundred pounds of cotton was a full day's work for Louise, while her husband could pick three hundred to four hundred pounds on a good day.[4]

Minnie Lee remembered wearing a sunbonnet as she worked on the East Texas farm her family owned, on which they primarily grew cotton but also grew food crops such as corn, sugar cane, sweet potatoes, and peanuts.[5]

The outfit for a white female cotton laborer in the early twentieth century generally included a sunbonnet and a long-sleeved dress or long-sleeved shirt with overalls. Betty Jumper remembers her grandmother, "in her bonnets, long dresses, cotton stockings, and dipping snuff."[6] As early as the 1910s, some American women had adopted the practical bib overall for their work clothing.[7] Beginning in the teens and twenties and continuing into the 1930s, striped overalls became popular for women, in color combinations such as blue and white, gray and black, black and red, and brown and white.[8] Louise recalled a pair of blue and white striped cotton overalls that she wore for cotton field work in the 1930s. These overalls contained dark blue and white stripes about one-fourth inch wide. The overalls were unique and special in her wardrobe as, unlike most of her clothes, they were purchased ready-made.[9]

Minnie Lee also had a pair of store-bought overalls, which she wore when working in the fields. Minnie Lee noted that she did the same work as a man in the cotton fields: "I worked just like my daddy did. I didn't ever mind working."[10] Minnie Lee's twenty-first-century memories mirror feelings sociologist Margaret Jarman Haygood found common among white Southern tenant farm women in 1939:

> In the matter of work preference, an overwhelming majority—seven-eighths—of the mothers like field work . . . better than housework. . . . These general statements were sometimes elaborated by descriptions of their bringing up—"We was most all girls and had to do field work just like boys," or contrariwise, "I was the only girl and worked just like a boy with my brothers." There is a great deal of pride in the ability to work like a man.[11]

Historian David Hackett Fischer traces these continuing twentieth-century attitudes toward gender and field work back to the British origins of the Scotch-Irish:

> Travelers in the backcountry [in the United States South] often reported that men and women routinely shared the heaviest manual labor. Both sexes worked together in the fields, not

Fig. 11. Louise Rusk (right) as a young woman, c.1930.
Personal collection of Louise Rusk.

merely at harvest time but through the entire growing season. . . . Those customs have sometimes been explained as a response to the frontier environment. But they did not exist in quite the same way on the Puritan frontier, and the same patterns had long been observed by travelers in the borderlands of North Britain.[12]

Any garment worn in the cotton fields was sure to quickly accumulate a layer of grime from the dirt and perspiration. Louise remembered that her family washed their slat bonnets along with the rest of the washing: "Back then, if we did a laundry once a week, we did well. You know, it was a task to draw your water and boil them in a wash pot."[13] In many families, a laundry day was held every one to two weeks, and sunbonnets would have been washed then.[14] Rural Texas families did laundry manually in the early twentieth century, as they did not possess washing machines.[15] Faye did not mind washing day: "I always liked washing, because you didn't have to go to the field. It took all of us to wash."[16] The laundry process was harsh, and sunbonnets had to be made of extremely sturdy materials to survive the boiling and scrubbing.

The wash day process was also dangerous: one former sharecropper from Texas recalled, "Everybody know of some kid, black or white, who got killed by falling in boiling wash pot."[17] Despite the difficulty of maintaining garments used for agricultural manual labor, a neat appearance was considered well worth the effort for the feeling of respectability this gave, even in circumstances of poverty. In Erskine Caldwell's 1932 novel of Southern poor whites, *Tobacco Road*, the character Ada Lester recalls with pride that her daughter "used to tell me how pretty I looked when I combed my hair of mornings and put on a clean apron and sunbonnet."[18]

Sunbonnets were primarily outdoor garments and were not worn inside the house. A sunbonnet would be taken off when a woman came inside from a day's work. Louise Rusk did this for as long as she was able to go outdoors to work in her yard and garden, hanging her sunbonnet on a peg just inside her door on the back screened porch when she came inside.[19] Some families hung their sunbonnets up on a nail inside the house. These nails might be located in the hallway or in a bedroom. Minnie Lee remembered that the nail where she hung her sunbonnet was in the "heater room," a room named for the wood heater within.[20] Faye recalled that her family had a "bonnet rack, right under the men's hat rack" in the hallway of her house.[21]

During the Great Depression, government-sponsored photographers documented agricultural workers across the country through the FSA photography project. The FSA was one of many New Deal programs designed to support workers during the Depression. A memorandum from Roy Emerson Stryker to

Fig. 12. An unlined slat sunbonnet, worn with the ties
unfastened. Dorothea Lange, "Migratory woman, originally
from Texas. Yakima Valley, Washington," August 1939,
Library of Congress, Prints and Photographs Division, FSA-OWI Collection,
LC-USF34-020287-E DLC (b&w film nitrate neg.).

Fig. 13. The ease of laundering a slat sunbonnet was crucial in a migrant workers' camp. This slat sunbonnet wearer stands in front of laundry tools, including a scrub board. Dorothea Lange, "Texas woman in carrot pullers' camp. Imperial Valley, California. The sunbonnet is typical of women who came from Texas," February 1939,
Library of Congress, Prints and Photographs Division,
FSA-OWI Collection, LC-USF34-019292-E DLC (b&w film nitrate neg.).

photographers in the project urged them to photograph various scenarios showing "American Background," including,

> People on and off the job . . . The effect of the depression in the smaller towns of the United States . . . Relationship between density of population and income of [sic] such things as Pressed clothes Polished shoes and so on [sic] Is it likely that in large industrial areas that even the poor groups will make a greater effort to have polished shoes, pressed clothes, than the same of even a higher-income group might in the smaller populated areas. [sic] What effect does wealth have on this?[22]

In response to these instructions, photographers such as Dorothea Lange and Russell Lee captured many images of women working outside in their distinctively rural working dress, which included sunbonnets. The captions photographers gave their photographs provide valuable information as to the context of the sunbonnets shown.

At the same time, this "come as you are party" of images presents an interesting power dynamic. We have on one hand an administrative arm of the United States government acting as patron of the art created and in many ways mandating the content of the images. The resulting photographs are like the genre paintings of previous centuries, unapologetic views of everyday life in all its glory. On the other hand, some of these images almost seem to

Fig. 14. The brim, flat crown, and tail of this slat sunbonnet are constructed from a single, continuous length of fabric. Dorothea Lange, "Cotton picking in South Texas," February 1936, Library of Congress, Prints and Photographs Division, FSA-OWI Collection, LC-USF34-009811-E DLC (b&w film nitrate neg.).

Fig. 15. A side view of the same slat sunbonnet wearer shown
in Fig. 4. Russell Lee, "Bunching carrots,
Edinburg, Texas," February 1939,
Library of Congress, Prints and Photographs Division, FSA-OWI Collection,
LC-USF33-011974-M5 DLC (b&w film nitrate neg.).

reach the level of propaganda with their socialist agenda of empowering "the people" or "the workers" at the expense of the agency of the individuals pictured.

Then there are the photographers, artists who no doubt were extremely glad to have employment in such difficult times that still allowed them to make art, and somewhat more freely than in a commercial context. The photographer serves as "the viewer, the active agent (the 'one who looks') choosing and controlling what is seen."[23] Many of the photographs seem to express a tremendous amount of empathy on the part of the viewer/photographer for the sunbonnet wearer/object of the images; at the same time, it must be acknowledged that for the photographers, even for a female photographer such as Lange, these women in their sunbonnets remain "Other." There is a barrier of privilege between the working woman harvesting turnips or picking cotton and the working woman whose tool is a camera, and who exerts agency in the framing of images.

Finally, there are the objects of the images, the sunbonnet wearers: I compare these photographic images to a "come as you are party" because many of the FSA images capture these women as they would have never presented themselves when exerting their own agency in front of the camera's eye. Some FSA images do show the viewed/object of the images as they might have chosen to be pictured: proud town women posed and displaying rows of neat jam jars in their modern, sanitary kitchens, for example. However, in my research, I have not run across any photograph from the early twentieth century owned by a sunbonnet wearer and showing her *in her sunbonnet and work clothes.* Instead, when sunbonnet wearers exerted agency in the creation of the photograph by choosing their own clothes and how they wished to be portrayed, they presented themselves in their best, most fashionable clothes. This seems to be a holdover from nineteenth-century photographic conventions. As author Claudia Kidwell notes:

> Painted portraits had for centuries shown subjects dressed in fine clothing. . . . This convention seems still to have been generally accepted in the mid-nineteenth century, and no doubt many sitters chose to appear in their very best clothing, with appropriate jewelry, accessories, and carefully styled hair.[24]

The image of Louise as a young woman circa 1930 (Fig. 11), for example, shows her in a fashionable dress and hat . . . even if the most elegant backdrop she could find was a stone wall. As a young cotton laborer, this ensemble would not have represented Louise as she appeared on most days; instead it shows her as she imagined herself and wished to be remembered. Art historian Anne Hollander asserts, "[D]ressing is an act usually undertaken with reference to pictures—mental pictures, which are personally edited versions of actual ones."[25] Hollander's fashion theory was actually

Fig. 16. The construction of this slat sunbonnet is very similar to that of "A Very Simple Slat Sunbonnet from the 1940s" shown in the Appendix; a center-back seam in the flat crown creates a peak, which is then tacked down. Dorothea Lange, "Wife of a Texas tenant farmer. The wide lands of the Texas Panhandle are typically operated by white tenant farmers, i.e., those who possess teams and tools and some managerial capacity," June 1937, *Library of Congress, Prints and Photographs Division, FSA-OWI Collection, LC-USF34-016945-E DLC (b&w film nitrate neg.).*

Fig. 17. The high crown of this poke-style sunbonnet
recalls that of the fashionable bonnets of the 1830s.
Russell Lee, "Woman washing her clothes on
her farm at El Indio, Texas," March 1939,
Library of Congress, Prints and Photographs Division, FSA-OWI
Collection, LC-USF33-012098-M1 DLC (b&w film nitrate neg.).

anticipated years before by the couturière Lucile (Lucy, Lady Duff Gordon, 1863–1935), who wrote in 1932, "All women make pictures for themselves, they go to the theatre and see themselves as the heroine of the play, they watch Marlene Dietrich or Greta Garbo acting for them at the cinema, but it is themselves they are watching really."[26] For the sunbonnet wearers I have interviewed, the dreary reality of work clothes and sunbonnet was not part of the mental picture of themselves that they nurtured in their own imaginations. Nor was this the way they wished to present themselves to others.

Ironically for the researcher, then, the most helpful primary materials from the early twentieth century are often those that capture sunbonnet wearers as "Othered" object of the photographer's gaze, and celebrate the working status that they would have preferred to leave behind. In these FSA photographs, we see sunbonnets in context: in the fields, the chicken-yard, the migrant camp in California. Rather than seeing the sunbonnet as an independent item of millinery, detached from the rest of the outfit and removed from the human body, we see these bonnets at work, as they were really worn.

The Depression forced many agricultural workers to migrate in search of work, and as they traveled, they took their sunbonnet styles, and the ideals of beauty inherent in these, with them. FSA photographers noted that the women from Texas continued to wear their slat bonnets, whether in camps in Washington state (Fig. 12) or pulling carrots in California (Fig. 13). These photographs make it clear why for many sunbonnet wearers the sunbonnet did retain associations with poverty and hard times.

FSA photographs document that sunbonnets were worn in the 1930s in other regions of Texas besides East Texas. These photographs show workers wearing slat sunbonnets while working in cotton and carrot fields in South Texas (Figs. 14 and 15), as well as tenant farmers wearing their slat sunbonnets in the broad fields of West Texas (Fig. 16). A West Texas woman washes her clothes outside, wearing a poke-style sunbonnet with a ruffle around the brim and a very high crown, echoing the shape of fashionable bonnets of the 1830s (Fig. 17). These photographs also show women wearing work clothes such as those described by the East Texas women: long-sleeved shirts with overalls and long-sleeved dresses are seen on women actually in the fields working.

Field workers were not the only women to wear sunbonnets in the early twentieth century in East Texas. Even women who lived in the company towns associated with sawmills and the lumber industry wore sunbonnets when they worked outside in the little gardens surrounding their company-owned housing.[27]

Later in the twentieth century, poke-style quilted brim sun-

Fig. 18. Convertible sunbonnet
and clothespin bag (apron),
made by Louise Jenkins Rusk in
2000. Shown as sunbonnet.
Author's collection.
Photograph by the author.

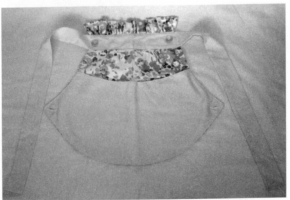

Fig. 19. Convertible sunbonnet and clothespin bag (apron), made by Louise
Jenkins Rusk in 2000. Shown as apron. Author's collection.
Photograph by the author.

bonnets with narrower brims became more popular.[28] This narrow sunbonnet brim is probably linked to the decline of hand picking of cotton, which had required laborers to work long days in full sunlight. Beginning in 1947, however, machinery began to replace workers who picked cotton by hand. By 1971 Texas cotton harvesting was entirely by machine.[29] The women wearing their sunbonnets in East Texas after World War II were more likely to be watering their flower beds or picking tomatoes for their own table rather than picking cotton. Yet many women whose youth had coincided with the Great Depression continued to wear the sunbonnet throughout the twentieth century.

Sunbonnets not only persisted into the twentieth century but also continued to evolve into new styles. Folklorist Janet K. Jeffery mentions a style of poke bonnet in which the brim is buttoned to the crown, and when unbuttoned forms a clothespin bag (clothespin apron). A sunbonnet in the author's collection (Figs. 18 and 19), made by Louise in 2000 of fabric most likely dating from the 1970s, falls into this category.[30] Jeffery states this sunbonnet style appeared during the 1980s.[31] Writer and apron collector Joyce Cheney, on the other hand, dates this design to the 1950s, and notes that such sunbonnet/apron combinations were sometimes given as gifts, such as one example that was found with a handwritten rhyme in its pocket: "I'm an apron as you can see / Button me up, I'm a bonnet cute as can be."[32] Star Caldwell of Arkansas has a similar sunbonnet pattern, which her grandmother wore in the 1930s. The Caldwell sunbonnet also makes the transformation from sunbonnet to apron; however, it utilizes multiple staves rather than having two simple pockets. Why make a sunbonnet that, when one comes indoors, can be converted into a rather small and nonfunctional apron? Novelty seems to be the primary motivator for this innovation and suggests that when and where this sunbonnet style is popular, as in rural East Texas in the 1980s, the sunbonnet has already passed out of the realm of necessity.

Why a Sunbonnet? Narrators' Reasons

In my oral history research, one of the most important questions that I asked each narrator was why she chose to wear a sunbonnet. It was important to me to elucidate not just the obvious reasons, but also perhaps reasons that had not been published previously. Additionally, it was important to give these women a voice—that my research be not just a "reading" of the sunbonnet in which I alone imputed meaning to the objects, but that it would also make use of the opportunity to let the sunbonnet wearers speak for themselves.

East Texas women of the twentieth century wore sunbonnets for year-round protection from extremes of weather, both heat and cold.[1] Minnie Lee noted that the main reason for wearing a sunbonnet was "to protect your face from the hot sun."[2] Her response suggests that the sunbonnet actually serves a twofold purpose, meeting both the physical need for cool shade and the aesthetic and social need to prevent the tanning of the skin. Julia agreed, noting that the primary reason for wearing a sunbonnet was "to keep the sun off" and to prevent "blistering."[3] Prior to the introduction of UV-blocking sunscreen products, the only sure way to avoid the discomfort of sunburn was to avoid prolonged sun exposure.

Opinions vary as to how comfortable it is to wear a sunbonnet. Some women found the limited field of vision—"like blinders"—uncomfortable.[4] For these women, wearing the sunbonnet made them feel not dissimilar to the family mule so often used to plow the fields in the days before tractors, with blinders to keep it focused on the physical labor at hand. In considering the way sunbonnets limited the wearer's vision, however, it should be pointed out that in addition to protecting the skin, the shade offered by sunbonnets also protected the wearer's eyes. Lace makers of centuries past might have gradually lost vision from working fine details in dim conditions, but early twentieth-century cotton workers spending all day in the glare of the southern sun prior to the availability of UV protective sunglasses could have also suffered vision damage in the production of textile goods.

There was also the debate of protection versus air circulation.

One 1916 British home study guide in sewing summed it up this way: "Some persons object to bonnets on the ground that they are too warm, and prefer sun hats; others, on the contrary, like the protection that sunbonnets give and for this reason prefer them."[5] The sunhat was very similar to a sunbonnet, but without ties under the chin, and usually without a tail. This allowed for cool breezes to reach the wearer, but did not fully prevent the sun's rays from doing the same. For Minnie Lee, wearing a sunbonnet was comfortable as it kept the wearer cooler while she worked.[6] Julia, on the other hand, said the tail of the sunbonnet made wearing one hot.[7] Faye thought sunbonnets were hotter and less comfortable than wearing a hat, because the closeness of the brim sides prevents air circulation.[8]

It is interesting that many women who enjoyed sunbonnets liked them for precisely this characteristic of wind protection. Eileen, who also makes and wears crocheted caps, said she prefers to wear a sunbonnet when she works outdoors in the winter because it keeps the wind out of her ears.[9] Faye's grandmother wore a sunbonnet for wind protection, claiming she did not "want the wind to get on her face."[10] Faye noted that the main reason for wearing a sunbonnet was to prevent sunburn: "They'd protect you all right. But they were miserable!"[11]

Louise enjoyed wearing a sunbonnet when she worked outside. She said sunbonnets are comfortable "if you don't tie them too tight. . . . Don't bother you at all." Louise preferred sunbonnets to hats. She found a sunbonnet easier to wear because its compact design and snug ties make a sunbonnet less likely to come off when working in windy conditions. This was especially important during her years in West Texas, where strong wind and sandstorms put any headgear at risk of blowing away. Louise noted that a wide-brimmed hat could shade a woman's face as well as a sunbonnet and possibly better than some of the later, narrow-brimmed sunbonnet styles. Nevertheless, she preferred to wear a sunbonnet.[12]

One of the more interesting responses to my question about whether she prefers a sunbonnet or a hat came from Julia, and offers an example of the intersection in the history of fashionable millinery and sunbonnets, even in the twentieth century. Julia replied, "I'd rather have a bonnet because a hat mashes your hair. . . . I used to wear my hair with curls all on top. . . . I would hate for it to get all mashed down. . . . A hat just mashes your hair all down."[13] While a few women thought sunbonnets could also be "hard on your hair," they were certainly less destructive to a hairstyle than a hat.[14] This may be a key factor in older East Texas women's choice to wear a sunbonnet rather than a hat for outdoor work in the mid- to late twentieth century.

American women in the post–World War II period made weekly trips to a salon to have their hair "set" in short, curly styles, and later short bouffant styles.[15] These hairstyles were reinforced with layers of hairspray to hold the style through the entire week. Older white women in East Texas continued wearing these styles throughout the century, even as fashions in hairstyles changed for younger women. It is precisely this genre of hairstyle to which Julia refers.

The fit of a hat usually involves a circle around the head where the weight of the hat is placed, and a straw hat must fit snugly to the head at this point in order to stay on the wearer, even if it also utilizes ties or an elastic band around the chin. This can create a "hat-head" effect of flattened hair or a line in the hair when the hat is removed. The "hat-head" effect became a major fashion dilemma for women in the mid-twentieth century when hairstyles began edging out hats in fashion importance, but hats were still required by etiquette for most occasions. New York milliner Lilly Daché responded to the crisis by designing hats that allowed a woman's hairstyle to be seen.[16] In 1958 the New York Times quoted Daché as asserting, "Big, deep hats that slide down to the ears are killing the millinery business. Women will not buy them because they do not want to cover up and crush their pretty hairdos."[17] First Lady Jacqueline Kennedy's hairdresser, Kenneth Battelle, noted that Mrs. Kennedy expressed a concern about hats similar to Julia's: "[S]he . . . didn't want her hair to get flattened out."[18]

While Mrs. Kennedy ultimately found her solution in small hats placed far back on her head, for East Texas women who wished to preserve both their twentieth-century hairstyles and their nineteenth-century-style complexions, the sunbonnet was an inexpensive and effective solution for outdoor work. The fit of a sunbonnet, unlike a hat, primarily depends on how tightly its ties are fastened under the chin, putting less pressure on the wearer's head—and hairstyle. It is logical, therefore, that older women who wore teased and sprayed hairstyles that had to last until the next salon appointment would choose the sunbonnet as a form of working headgear.

The Sunbonnet and White Skin

So what does the sunbonnet tell us about American society? The sunbonnet, an object both fabricated by and used by American women in rural areas, reveals some of their beliefs about what makes a woman beautiful and socially acceptable. In the twentieth-century sunbonnet, the nineteenth-century ideal of the beautiful female body is preserved, with its biased emphasis on white skin.

The link between pale skin and beauty is codified even within the English language itself. The first definition given for the word fair by the *American Heritage College Dictionary* is: "Of pleasing appearance . . . comely." The second definition is (a) "Light in color, especially blonde: fair hair," and (b) "Of light complexion: fair skin." Thus we see the linguistic link between beauty and whiteness that was passed down to rural working-class white women of East Texas at the beginning of the twentieth century.

White skin was idealized for centuries in Europe. By the end of the sixteenth century, fashionable European women were whitening both their faces and their breasts using hazardous lead-based cosmetics and borax.[1] In the eighteenth century, women of fashion still used whitening cosmetics, although the availability of smallpox inoculations meant that fewer women needed thick layers of paint to cover scars left by the disease. Makeup became less toxic, and pearl powder was a new way to achieve a white complexion.[2] The nineteenth century continued the vogue for white skin, although for respectable women the emphasis moved from cosmetic enhancement to tanning prevention, assisted by the proliferation of fashionable bonnet styles that kept the sunlight at bay.[3]

In 1896, British novelist Elinor Glyn summarized what made an unattractive complexion by nineteenth-century standards, as she harshly judged the appearance of the other women being presented at Court with her: "There were numbers of hideous women there, with—Ye Gods—what skins. Brown or pimply, or red and coarse."[4] A darker complexion was considered a problem, as unforgivable as acne, and tellingly associated with the "coarseness" of working people. As Edmonde Charles-Roux noted, "Whereas a milky skin seemed a sure sign of aristocracy, a tanned one could indicate nothing but modest or plebian origins."[5] The social and economic theorist Thorstein Veblen, writing in 1899, skewered the fashionable world's pursuit of a languorous type of beauty: "Our dress, therefore, in order to serve its purpose effectually, should not only be expensive, but it should also make plain to all observers that the wearer is not engaged in any kind of productive labor."[6] Skin tone was as much a part of a fashionable white woman's toilette as was her dress, and it was just as important in establishing her position as a nonlaborer.

White skin, as fair as possible, was the goal for nineteenth-century Caucasian women with any pretension to leisure. They were aided in this pursuit by a variety of beauty treatments that claimed to lighten skin, remove freckles, and otherwise counteract the effects of sun exposure.[7] There was but a single standard of fashionable beauty, and it inherently discriminated against women of color and working women. In the nineteenth century, in the frontier region of the American plains, Laura Ingalls Wilder's mother, Caroline, chided her daughters, "'I declare . . . if you girls aren't getting to look like Indians! Can I never teach you to keep your sunbonnets on?'"[8] For this nineteenth-century mother, a suntan was not just unattractive, not just an uncomfortable similarity to a race deemed inferior; it was "uncivilized"—a capitulation to the hardships and realities of frontier life, which she sought to ward off through the sunbonnet.

The nineteenth-century ideal did not vanish with the turning of the century. Faye remembered that in the early twentieth century her mother gave her an admonishment similar to that of Caroline Ingalls: "'Close those doors when you go out, and get that bonnet! You're going to ruin your skin. And you won't be able to go out in the world from being out in the sunbeams too much.'"[9] Embedded in Faye's mother's warning is a similar concern about using the sunbonnet to protect a semblance of refinement; she feared that skin tanned by the sun would serve to limit her daughter's opportunities in the world beyond the cotton fields.

Folklore columnist Pearl Lowe Boyd recalled being scolded for many abuses of her sunbonnet, several of which involved removing it: "Bonnets also caused little girls to receive lots of scoldings: . . . for wearing them tied under the chin but swinging down the back, for carrying wild strawberries, blackberries, juicy peaches, and other runny, staining articles therein, and for leaving them in some unrecalled spot."[10]

Louise did not wear her sunbonnet regularly until she was a young woman of fourteen, three years before she would be married. Louise explained why it was more important to wear a sunbonnet as a young woman than it was as a child: "[Y]ou wanted to take care of your complexion better. You wanted to look better by that time. Started growing up, you know. . . . I didn't take care of myself until I got to be a teenager."[11]

As a rural white woman neared adulthood, it became impor-

Fig. 20. Both slat sunbonnets and kerchiefs were worn by the
Mexican American women shown here. Russell Lee, "Mexican
girl, carrot worker, Edinburg, Texas," February 1939,
Library of Congress, Prints and Photographs Division, FSA-OWI Collection,
LC-USF33-011974-M1 DLC
(b&w film nitrate neg.).

tant for her to conform to the community's standard of beauty and to comport herself with accepted notions of propriety in order to appeal to the opposite sex. "Looking better" meant looking paler. Despite the economic reality that working-class rural farm women had to participate in the agricultural labor and output of the farm, or perhaps precisely *because* of this reality, pallor was associated with increased femininity and attractiveness. Marriage and the family structure was more than a moral imperative; it was also an economic necessity for survival. A woman needed to find a spouse and pursuing the accepted forms of beauty in her rural community were part and parcel of that project. The ideal beauty was still the delicate white beauty of the nineteenth century, ignoring the changes in ideal complexion that the twentieth century was bringing.

One of the essences of fashion is that its standards change and are continually evolving in the quest for novelty. After World War I, leaders of Paris fashion such as Gabrielle "Coco" Chanel had promoted sunbathing, and by 1923 fashionable women were venturing to the beach without hats.[12] According to author Philippe Perrot, "From then on tanning was integral to a new field of significative oppositions, so that in the twentieth century it symbolize[d] exactly what 'milky-white skin' had signified in the nineteenth: idleness, or the economic ability to waste time 'doing nothing' and to display this gratifying unproductiveness."[13] What female golfers had not yet been prepared to accept in the very earliest years of the century was now the fashion; a tan was the new mark of the leisured class.

Another key principle of fashion is that whatever is most difficult to obtain or maintain is likely to be the most desirable from a fashionable point of view.[14] Even Chanel (who had come from a less-than-privileged background) continued covering her hands to avoid looking like a manual laborer.[15] For rural East Texas white women who really did work with their hands in the fields, this same impulse prevented them from embracing the suntan, even while they embraced other aspects of the current fashions. For example, a sunbonnet of the 1920s might cover a head of fashionably bobbed hair. For those picking cotton, a suntan evoked labor, not leisure, and it was whiteness, not a tan, that was most difficult to maintain. At age ninety-one, Louise was still uninterested in a suntan. "I'm dark enough already, without getting any darker," she said of her olive complexion.[16]

Interestingly, Faye noted that sunbonnets also prevented the hair from being sun-bleached. Sun-bleached hair was undesirable, as it was another tell-tale sign that a person had been working outdoors.[17]

Anglo women were not the only sunbonnet wearers. Mexican American women of the 1930s also wore sunbonnets when working in the fields of South Texas. FSA photographs document

Mexican American women working in either deep slat sunbonnets or large kerchiefs (Fig. 20).

The great variety of skin tones within the Mexican American community has coexisted with a history of some skin colors being privileged over others at different points in time. In stanza six of her poem "We Would Like You to Know," Ana Castillo writes,

> We would like you to know
> we are not all brown.
> Genetic history has made
> some of us blue eyed as any
> German immigrant
> and as black as a descendant
> of an African slave.
> We never claimed to be
> a homogenous race.[18]

In his book *When We Arrive*, José F. Aranda, Jr., notes, "In the heyday of the Chicano/a Movement, one couldn't be 'güero' (a person of Mexican descent who looks or passes for white) and be 'authentically' Chicano/a. . . . [B]ronze skin was one of the essential pre-conditions for membership in la raza."[19] The early Chicano/a movement's choice of which skin colors to privilege within their community was a way of subverting previous ideals of beauty representing oppression (external and internal) in a preference for lighter skin tones. Over most of American history, mestizos (individuals of mixed Spanish and indigenous ancestry) received better legal treatment than Native Americans,[20] and even within the mestizo community greater status was enjoyed by those of lighter skin.[21]

It is interesting to note that even in the second half of the twentieth century, a Mexican American *man* recalls receiving a warning about sun exposure remarkably similar to that given to Faye and Louise. Richard Rodriguez records in his autobiography that his mother scolded him when he remained outside in the sun too long, saying, "'You won't be satisfied till you end up looking like *los pobres* who work in the fields, *los braceros.*'"[22] Even for a man late in the twentieth century, a dark skin tone could indicate the low status of an agricultural manual laborer, looked down on by a racist and classist dominant culture. How much more so, then, would this have affected Mexican American women of the early twentieth century? It is likely that the Mexican American farm women shown in the FSA photographs selected sunbonnets for reasons similar to those of their Anglo counterparts: to secure whatever small increase in societal status was afforded by a lighter complexion.

Folklorist Janet K. Jeffery both captures some truth and oversimplifies the complexity of the racial implications of the sunbonnet when she writes, "A symbol of the white pioneering

Fig. 21. The brim of this sunbonnet or sunhat is soft enough
to be folded back. "Gathering Eggs." 1930. Agricultural
Communications Office of the Texas Agricultural Extension
Service Archives, reference number 001007001.
*Courtesy Cushing Memorial Library and Archives, Texas A&M University, and
the Texas AgriLife Extension Service.*

woman, the sunbonnet's very function was to preserve a woman's ethnic identity in an age when varying shades of skin locked a person into certain social and economic strata. By contrast, black women preferred to wear turbans or bandanas."[23] While many African American women did wear turban-style headcoverings or straw hats, there is clear evidence that they also sometimes wore sunbonnets, particularly in the nineteenth century.[24]

In Helen Bradley Foster's analysis of antebellum clothing described by former slaves or their descendants for the Federal Writers' Project (FWP) of 1936–1938, she notes that four types of head coverings were mentioned: headrags, hats, caps, and bonnets.[25] One narrator cited by Foster, Georgia Telfair, reported, "Us wore homespun dresses wid bonnets to match. De bonnets wuz all made in one piece an' had drawstrings on de back to make 'em fit, an' slats in de brims to make 'em stiff an' straight."[26] (Note that the dialect here is as transcribed by the interviewers in the 1930s). This description sounds exactly like the easy-care slat bonnet that can be sewn from a single, rectangular piece of fabric, with exterior ties attached to adjust the fit, which Hispanic and Anglo farm women continued to wear into the twentieth century.

Fashion historian Gerilyn Tandberg also cites a Georgia slave narrative for evidence that some African American women did indeed wear sunbonnets. This narrator describes wearing a white pique poke-style dress sunbonnet, stiffened using flour starch.[27]

If African American women were less likely to wear sunbonnets as the twentieth century unfolded, perhaps narrator Hanna Fambro's story sheds some light on possible reasons why:

> De sunbonnets dey was made . . . wid long tales [sic] that come ovah de shouldahs like a cape. Dey tied undah de chin, an' 'bout noonday dose sunbonnets ud make us so hot and keep off so much air dat we'd open de strings an tie 'em on de top of our heads. Then us ud take de tail a little bit from 'round our neck. But ef we see de ole man comin' we'd drop 'em in a hurry 'cause he'd whip us ef he ketch dose tales up. You see, he 'fraid to have us get brain fever.[28]

Fambro's memory of being forced to wear especially stifling sunbonnets during slavery—with personal comfort and protection being sacrificed to the owner's drive to protect his "investment" from perceived health threats—offers at least one explanation for why the sunbonnet might not have been a first choice for rural African American women in later years. Any garment associated with slavery was certain to be less appealing, especially for darker-skinned women who were not as easily damaged by sun exposure.

However, African American women did sometimes wear sunbonnets, through the end of the nineteenth century and into the twentieth century. At the Paris Exposition Universelle in 1900, W. E. B. (William Edward Burghardt) DuBois (1868–1963) exhibited

Fig. 22. Sunbonnets coexisted with fashionable hairstyles, such as the bob worn by this African American woman. "Poultry House and Flock of Barred Rocks." 1930. Agricultural Communications Office of the Texas Agricultural Extension Service Archives, reference number 001006001.
Courtesy Cushing Memorial Library and Archives, Texas A&M University, and the Texas AgriLife Extension Service.

photograph albums of African Americans in Georgia. His exhibit included a photograph of three women and one man hoeing in a field; while one of the women wears a headwrap, two of the women wear sunbonnets with very full crowns.[29]

One interesting twentieth-century photograph of an African American woman wearing a sunhat or a sunbonnet is a part of the Agricultural Communications Office of the Texas Agricultural Extension Service archive (Fig. 21). In this 1930 photograph, a Mrs. O. M. Polk of Houston, Texas, is shown gathering eggs from her henhouse, pairing her sunbonnet with a cotton print, wrapper-style dress. Her hat may not be technically a sunbonnet, as it does not appear to have front ties to hold it on the head, but its shape is very similar to the brim and crown of a sunbonnet. It lacks a tail, but does have a sunbonnet-like drawstring feature that pulls in the fullness of the crown at the back of the head. The poke-style brim is not starched stiffly, and Mrs. Polk has turned the brim back— whether to improve her vision inside the henhouse, or just to show her face for the photograph, we do not know. The underside of the brim is a contrasting fabric, light in color.

The archive also contains a second photograph of Mrs. Polk (Fig. 22). In this image she is posing outside the henhouse, holding her sunbonnet in her hands. With the sunbonnet removed, we can see that she sports a smart bobbed hairstyle; this demonstrates that as with white farming women, African American farming women's hairstyles might keep up with contemporary fashions even as headcoverings for work remained stagnant. The outside shot also shows a full-length view of Mrs. Polk's ensemble, with the surprising revelation that despite her sunhat and workaday dress, she is wearing stockings and pumps! As in the case with the FSA images of white cotton laborers, we must address the issue of who is taking the photograph, and the purpose the image was created to serve.

When looking at the FSA photographs, it is clear that while many were taken by artists observing people at work under their ordinary conditions, some are obviously posed (apron-clad women in pristine kitchens gesturing like game-show hostesses toward a pantry full of preserves). As a photograph taken by the Agricultural Communications Office of the Texas Agricultural Extension Agency, this photograph was probably taken to show a "success story" of a life improved through modern practices and agricultural education; the caption states that "Mrs. Polk markets and [sic] average of 50 dozen eggs per week. She owns ten acres of land and has owned it for five years. The place has been developed in the last three years; the land valued at $1500 and the buildings valued at $2000." It is possible that the photograph shows a balance struck between Mrs. Polk's desire to look nice for the camera (hence the stockings and pumps), and the photographer's desire for the subject seen in "Gathering Eggs" to look plausibly dressed for this activity—at least from the hemline up.

A 1954 image from Brazos County, Texas, shows an African American woman in a garden patch, wearing an almost helmet-like sunbonnet or sunhat (Fig. 23). The crown of this sunbonnet is tall (possibly supported by wire or doweling?) and the brim is narrow. As with Mrs. Polk's sunbonnet, this would offer some sun protection, but not the cavelike (and sometimes stifling) conditions of a large slat bonnet.

The conclusion we can draw from these photographs and oral histories is that African American women did in fact sometimes wear sunbonnets and perhaps sunbonnet-style sunhats. The pattern of millinery for outdoor work cannot be reduced to a simple white = sunbonnet / black = headwrap dichotomy, which overlooks other women of color (such as Mexican American sunbonnet wearers) completely and discounts the ability of individual women to exert agency even within limited economic circumstances through their choice of headgear.

While the sunbonnets worn in the Agricultural Communications Office photographs seem to offer less coverage than someone seeking to shield her skin color might have chosen, there were probably lighter-skinned African American women who wore sunbonnets to protect whatever advantages their lighter complexions might offer. In Talita Tademy's fictionalized account of her mixed-race, African American and French Creole family, she

Fig. 23. This African American woman wears a sunbonnet with a towering crown and a narrow brim that does not interfere with her vision. "Jim Williams Brazos County June 54 Sloan." 1954. Agricultural Communications Office of the Texas Agricultural Extension Service Archives.

Courtesy Cushing Memorial Library and Archives, Texas A&M University, and the Texas AgriLife Extension Service.

describes her great-grandmother Emily, able to pass for white, who in 1936 "wished she had on one of her serviceable long-billed bonnets, but she wouldn't wear them to town anymore since her granddaughter had told her they weren't fashionable. She wore a smaller bonnet, not as good to keep sun off, but a pretty little thing."[30]

The attitudes of women in the farming communities of East Texas suggest that rural Anglo women maintained the idea that white skin was beautiful well into the twentieth century, and the women who reached adulthood in the early years of the century tended to retain this view throughout their lives. Although slightly beyond the scope of the discussion here, it is also important to note that these women often retained a nineteenth-century view of the ideal weight, as well, preferring a more curvaceous figure rather than the "modern" body type slimmed by diet and exercise.[31] For farm laboring women, thinness would always be associated with poverty and hard manual labor, rather than with wealth, fashion, and leisure.

I can still remember my horror as a teenager in the early 1990s when my grandmother congratulated me on the whiteness of my legs. When she realized that I was not pleased by her compliment, she tried again by patting my leg and assuring me that at any rate, she was sure I had gained some weight and my legs looked plumper.

Among women like my grandmother in isolated rural areas of the United States, the sunbonnet persisted throughout the twentieth century as they held onto the ideals of beauty impressed upon them at an early age, even as they witnessed the twentieth century's many changes. In 2004, Faye expressed amazement about how the ideals of beauty changed during her lifetime, from pale to tan. "And now," Faye said, "I have a daughter—she takes everything she can off and goes into the backyard and gets all the sun she can!"[32]

Decline (and Revival?) of the Sunbonnet

In 1840 the ratio of Americans living in the country versus the city was 9:1. By 1900 this ratio had dropped to 3:2.[1] However, by the late 1870s, in the East Coast states of Massachusetts, Rhode Island, Connecticut, New York, and New Jersey, urban dwellers already exceeded those who lived in rural areas.[2] Changes that occurred within this taste-making region were bound to affect fashion and attitudes across the nation. While Texas remained a majority rural population into the 1940s, the sunbonnet was already beginning to develop somewhat negative associations among young women of East Texas even before Texas became an urban society.[3] However, the young women of the 1930s often continued wearing their sunbonnets for outdoor work throughout the twentieth century, even as they believed such bonnets to be unfashionable.

Folklorist Janet K. Jeffery wrote in 1993, "Now . . . toward the end of the twentieth century, elderly women hoeing their gardens in small Texas towns are the principal wearers of the American sunbonnet."[4] In the early years of the twenty-first century, the last generation of sunbonnet wearers is composed of women in their late eighties and nineties. When I interviewed Louise in 2004, she still wore a sunbonnet; until her death in 2008, she continued to wear a sunbonnet when she was able to go outside in her yard.[5] Faye stopped wearing her sunbonnet twenty to thirty years prior to our 2004 interview, in the 1970s or early 1980s; unfortunately, in our interview I did not ask her more specifically why she stopped wearing her sunbonnet.[6]

Sunbonnets ceased to be worn as they developed connotations of being old-fashioned, backward, and agrarian, as opposed to hats, which were considered modern, sophisticated, progressive, and urban. Faye told a story about going to a cemetery homecoming in Nacogdoches County, Texas. A cemetery homecoming was a special holiday-like day on which people returned to the cemetery where their ancestors were buried for a day of work and fellowship, cleaning the tombstones, tidying the grounds, putting out flowers, and often enjoying a picnic-style "dinner on the grounds" as well. At this homecoming Faye remembered seeing a

Plate 1. Lavender silk calash. Eighteenth century. *Collection of the Costume Institute, The Metropolitan Museum of Art, Gift of Art Worker's Club, 1945. (C.I.45.68.44). Image © The Metropolitan Museum of Art.*

Plate 2. Calico drawn bonnet. *Collection of the Costume Institute, The Metropolitan Museum of Art, Gift of Miss Irene Lewisohn, 1937. (C.I.37.56.149). Image © The Metropolitan Museum of Art.*

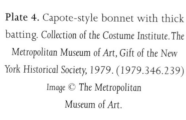

Plate 3. Capote-style bonnet with thick batting. *Texas Fashion Collection, 1965.039.003. Courtesy of the Texas Fashion Collection, College of Visual Arts, University of North Texas. Photograph by Andrea Hoback.*

Plate 4. Capote-style bonnet with thick batting. *Collection of the Costume Institute. The Metropolitan Museum of Art, Gift of the New York Historical Society, 1979. (1979.346.239) Image © The Metropolitan Museum of Art.*

Plate 5. Straw poke bonnet with fabric bavolet and chin ties. *Texas Fashion Collection, 1998.002.014. Courtesy of the Texas Fashion Collection, College of Visual Arts, University of North Texas. Photograph by Andrea Hoback.*

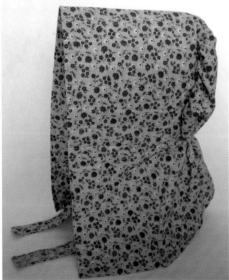

Plate 6. Yellow calico slat sunbonnet, twentieth century, East Texas. *Author's collection. Photograph by the author.*

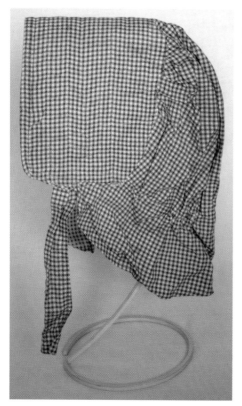

Plate 7. Lelia Evie Dorsett Rusk's green gingham poke-style field sunbonnet, with square pattern quilting on brim, probably early twentieth century. Nacogdoches County, Texas. *Private collection. Photograph by the author.*

Plate 8. Rounded silhouette poke-style sunbonnet in daisy print, twentieth century, East Texas. *Private collection. Photograph by the author.*

Plate 9. Blue cotton, wooden slat sunbonnet.
Carolina mountains, nineteenth century.
Collection of the Costume Institute,
The Metropolitan Museum of Art, Gift
of Miss Irene Lewisohn, 1938. (C.I. 38.96.4).
Image © The Metropolitan Museum of Art.

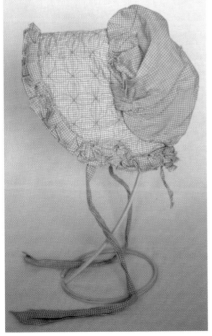

Plate 10. Ruby Isabelle Turner Duke's
blue gingham, rounded brim, poke-style
sunbonnet, with quilted interlocking
circles on brim, probably early twentieth
century, East Texas. Private collection.
Photograph by the author.

Plate 11. Blue "gingham" print, bill-shaped and unquilted brim, poke-style sunbonnet. East Texas. *Author's collection.* *Photograph by the author.*

Plate 12. Black cotton, poke-style sunbonnet with brim quilted in spiraling squares, late nineteenth century, Burnett, Texas. *Museum of Texas Tech University, MTTU 1955-79-1.*

Plate 13. Child's poke-style,
square-shaped brim sunbonnet;
brim hand-quilted
in parallelogram shapes,
mid-nineteenth century.
Museum of Texas Tech University,
MTTU 14230 1987-117-13.

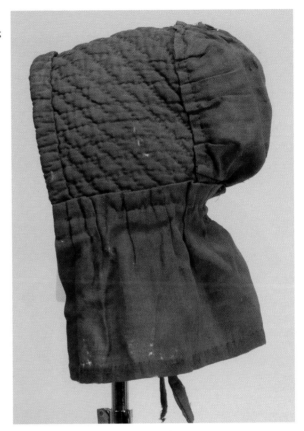

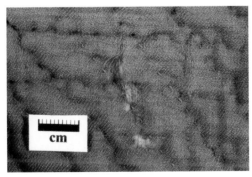

Plate 14. Detail of child's poke-style,
square-shaped brim sunbonnet
(Plate 13); brim hand-quilted in
parallelogram shapes,
mid-nineteenth century.
Museum of Texas Tech University,
MTTU 14230 1987-117-13.

Plate 15. Blue silk
sunbonnet, wholly hand-
quilted, with areas of loss
revealing batting. *Texas
Fashion Collection,*
1900.076.003. Courtesy of the
Texas Fashion Collection,
College of Visual Arts,
University of North Texas.
Photograph by
Andrea Hoback.

Plate 16. Detail of blue silk sunbonnet (Plate 15),
wholly hand-quilted, with areas of loss revealing
batting. *Texas Fashion Collection, 1900.076.003. Courtesy*
of the Texas Fashion Collection, College of Visual Arts,
University of North Texas.
Photograph by Andrea Hoback.

Plate 17. Silk taffeta, poke-style sunbonnet with brim quilted in both straight and intersecting lines. *Texas Fashion Collection, 1970.044.002. Courtesy of the Texas Fashion Collection, College of Visual Arts, University of North Texas. Photograph by Andrea Hoback.*

Plate 18. Black silk, poke-style sunbonnet with parallelogram shapes hand-quilted on brim. Outer brim edge is also supported by a wire. *Museum of Texas Tech University, MTTU 1963-50-16.*

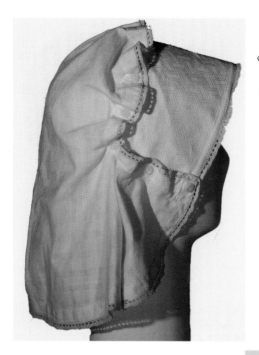

Plate 19. Off-white, square-brimmed, poke-style sunbonnet with buttoning, crenellated crown and tail, and crocheted trim. *Texas Fashion Collection, 1968.005.006. Courtesy of the Texas Fashion Collection, College of Visual Arts, University of North Texas. Photograph by Andrea Hoback.*

Plate 20. Blue cotton poke-style sunbonnet with lower crown crenellated through series of snaps; eyelet trim. *Texas Fashion Collection, 1900.028.002. Courtesy of the Texas Fashion Collection, College of Visual Arts, University of North Texas. Photograph by Andrea Hoback.*

Plate 21. Narrator Minnie Lee Skelton models a slat sunbonnet,
which she estimates to be from the 1930s.
Photograph by the author. 2002.

Plate 22. Brown linen slat sunbonnet, with pasteboard slats alternating with wooden dowels. American, c.1850. *Collection of the Costume Institute. The Metropolitan Museum of Art, Gift of Mrs.William R.Witherell, 1953. (C.I.53.72.24). Image © The Metropolitan Museum of Art.*

Plate 23. Detail of brown linen slat sunbonnet (Plate 22), with pasteboard slats alternating with wooden dowels. American, c.1850. *Collection of the Costume Institute. The Metropolitan Museum of Art, Gift of Mrs.William R.Witherell, 1953. (C.I.53.72.24). Image © The Metropolitan Museum of Art.*

Plate 24. Brown slat sunbonnet with buttoning, crenellated crown, long tail, and cuff at outer brim edge, late nineteenth or early twentieth century, West Texas. *Texas Fashion Collection, 1969.017.001. Courtesy of the Texas Fashion Collection, College of Visual Arts, University of North Texas. Photograph by Andrea Hoback.*

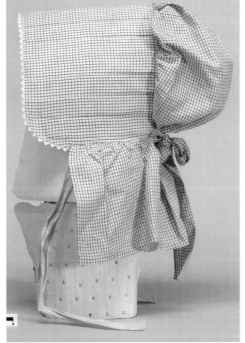

Plate 25. Black and white windowpane check slat sunbonnet, with contrasting pink brim lining, rick-rack trim. *Museum of Texas Tech University, MTTU 1249 1974-112-1.*

Plate 26. Blue chambray
poke-style sunbonnet with
tightly quilted brim, crown
with back horseshoe shape,
and puff, 14 1/2" tail.
Museum of Texas Tech University,
MTTU 1958-13-24.

Plate 27. Back view of blue chambray poke-style sunbonnet (Plate 26), showing resemblance to back of calash. *Museum of Texas Tech University,* MTTU 1958-13-24.

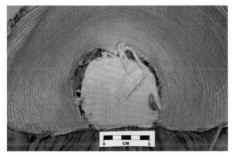

Plate 28. Detail of blue chambray poke-style sunbonnet (Plate 26), showing construction of crown interior. *Museum of Texas Tech University,* MTTU 1958-13-24.

Plate 29. This black silk twill entirely quilted dress bonnet has grosgrain ribbon ties. *Collection of the Costume Institute, The Metropolitan Museum of Art, Gift of Art Worker's Club, 1945. (C.I.45.68.131) Image © The Metropolitan Museum of Art.*

Plate 30. Calico poke-style sunbonnet with L-shaped quilting following line of brim; crown and tail in one continuous length of fabric. *Texas Fashion Collection, 1970.044.004. Courtesy of the Texas Fashion Collection, College of Visual Arts, University of North Texas. Photograph by Andrea Hoback.*

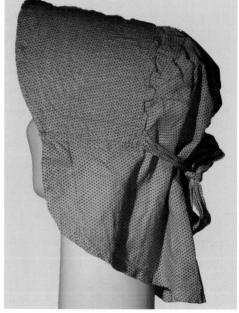

girl from Houston who wore a straw hat rather than a bonnet: "So I asked her, 'Where did you get that hat?' And she told me where she had bought it in Houston, and that it was seventy-five cents. So I said to my grandma and grandpa when I got home . . . 'Grandpa, I want to work for you. I want to make seventy-five cents, because I want a straw hat.'"[7]

Faye's grandfather gave her the herculean task of cutting all the bitter weeds in the hog pasture in order to earn the money, which was equal to one and a half days' pay in the cotton fields for a grown woman, as recalled by Louise.[8] But so strong was Faye's desire for the sophistication of a straw hat rather than a sunbonnet that she labored for two days before her grandfather gave in and gave her the money. This hat was then saved for special occasions, with her sunbonnet worn the rest of the time.[9] A straw hat represented the epitome of fashion for young Faye; the sunbonnet was simply rural costume.

In 1941, at the same time that Faye and Louise were young women in their late twenties wearing sunbonnets for all their outdoor work, the New York–based interior designer Dorothy Draper was busy publishing her cheerful tome *Entertaining Is Fun!: How to Be a Popular Hostess*, which presented her ideas "on making living fun" to a suburban and urban middle-class American audience.[10] Draper was so far removed from the realities of rural Southern agricultural life that to her the sunbonnet was an amusing and quaint garment springing from the pages of American history, rather than an item of daily living. One of Draper's ideas for Thanksgiving entertaining involved the sunbonnet as fancy dress, as she described a creative hostess welcoming her Thanksgiving guests "dressed like an old-fashioned farmer's wife in a prim pink calico dress and a starched apron and a sunbonnet."[11]

Similarly, a *Vogue* article of March 1954 treats its suburban and urban audience to a vision of sunbonnets as local color, in an article entitled "Roadside Holiday, U.S.A.": "In Wisdom [Kentucky], a clothesline nodded with patchwork quilts like square bright flowers. Lizzie Duff (opposite), in the crenellated bonnet she made, said, 'Don't people wear bonnets where you come from?'" (Fig. 5).[12] The assumption is, of course, that the modern fashionable woman who reads *Vogue* certainly does not wear a sunbonnet. While it is implied that Duff is naïve to think that her sartorial experiences are typical, the *Vogue* reader is reassured in her assumption that her urban life and manner of dress represent sophistication and modernity. In order for consumer culture to thrive and for seasonally changing mass-produced goods to replace home-crafted ones, it was necessary to imbue handcrafts such as sunbonnets with the stigma of being out-of-date, rustic, and antimodern, smacking of poverty and frontier subsistence existence. A sunbonnet might perhaps be fun for a theme party, but certainly not part of everyday life.

132

In the 1970s, perhaps sparked by the upcoming bicentennial celebrations of 1976, Americans across the country took up history as a hobby. Inspired by Georgia's Foxfire (founded 1966), high schools across the country became centers for oral history research. Many of these resulted in publications, such as *Bittersweet* and *Loblolly*, which recorded crucial information about the sunbonnet at a time when many narrators who had made and worn sunbonnets were still alive and active in their communities. Any research on the American sunbonnet today would have been much more difficult if not for this period of widespread interest in all things historical.

By the late twentieth century, not all sunbonnet wearers sewed their own bonnets or had someone in their family to sew for them. Some wearers purchased their sunbonnets from vendors, who sewed bonnets at home to sell. Church bazaars were one place where home-sewers sometimes sold the sunbonnets they made.[13] Other seamstresses sold sunbonnets at flea markets. In 2004 I spoke to one woman, Eileen, who sews poke-style sunbonnets and sells her wares at the Nacogdoches Trade Days flea market in Nacogdoches County, Texas.[14] Seventy-eight years old when I interviewed her, at that time Eileen could be found regularly at the monthly flea market, selling sunbonnets and crocheted items.

Although a longtime sunbonnet wearer, Eileen began making sunbonnets to sell to others in the early 1980s. At the time, her flea market booth centered on glass objects; she wore her sunbonnet to protect her ears on long days at the market. Eileen soon found that people were as interested in her sunbonnet as they were in her glass goods, and customers asked to buy a sunbonnet like hers. By 2004 her clientele had included both local customers who bought sunbonnets to wear themselves and tourists who bought her bonnets to take home as souvenirs to locations in Europe, Australia, and Asia.

Unlike the sunbonnets most East Texas women made for their own use in the early twentieth century, Eileen's sunbonnets are made from inexpensive, but new, materials. She shops for her fabrics at the Nacogdoches Wal-Mart, a twenty-four-hour behemoth of a store. There is no longer a dedicated fabric store in her town. While Eileen does use some simple all-cotton fabrics similar to those used early in the twentieth century, she now favors cotton/polyester blend calicoes, and uses perma-press materials if available. She sews with plain white Wal-Mart brand polyester thread, and notes that she always uses white thread because it is easier to see when she is sewing.

Eileen's sunbonnets are of the poke-style variety, with simple brims quilted in straight lines. She has experimented with a variety of stiffening materials over the years. At the beginning of her business, she cut up old sheets and used these as the layer between the outer fabric layers on the brim. She also tried using kraft paper for stiffening, but this "gathered up" in the sewing machine. At another point, she tried using a commercial interfacing on a batch of sunbonnets; however, she discovered too late that the interfacing needed to be preshrunk. When one of these bonnets that she had kept for herself buckled in the wash, she braced herself for a wave of returns . . . but no one did ask for a replacement. I suspect that her customers were either too polite to ask for a replacement or—more likely—that most of her customers had bought the sunbonnets as souvenirs rather than as work garb for themselves. In 2004 Eileen had settled on a plain, heavy fabric (possibly a canvas) for her stiffening material. She does not starch her stiffening layer before sewing it in the sunbonnets because the starch can cause the sunbonnets to crease if they "sit" for a while before selling.[15]

Today, the Internet provides a convenient way of sharing information about almost any topic, and the sunbonnet is no exception. There are multiple websites available that post articles with free sunbonnet patterns and sewing instructions.[16] One 1978 article by Betty Callahan, now available online, suggests a twist on the classic slat sunbonnet, using slats cut from a plastic milk jug. Callahan argues that with the traditional type of slat sunbonnet one "had to laboriously remove and reinsert the stiffeners each washday to keep them from getting soggy," and suggests that by sewing these plastic slats in permanently one can save time and effort.[17] Her use of the word "laborious" here truly illustrates the subjectivity of how we perceive the difficulty of housework—what was once considered a major labor- and time-saver (by eliminating the need for starching and ironing) is now labeled too difficult for the contemporary reader—and this was written thirty years ago. Callahan was thinking of and writing for a reader who was planning to use and wear her new sunbonnet on a regular basis, but I should also note here that plastic does create a range of conservation issues for anyone trying to preserve garments in a collection, and a plastic slat permanently sewn into a sunbonnet brim might damage the bonnet's fabric over time.

Just as sunbonnets made a brief and faddish appearance in the world of fashion around the turn of the twentieth century, they have also reappeared on the radar of the fashion world in the early years of the twenty-first century. During the New York spring/summer 2007 shows in the tents at Bryant Park, New Zealand fashion designer Karen Walker surprised editors and buyers by sending four sunbonnets down her runway. Walker's sunbonnets were shown in solid colors, over hair worn loose and long. The brims did not appear to be of the slat variety; irregular crease lines, different in each bonnet, suggested that the sunbonnets were stiffened through the thickness of fabric layers, perhaps in addition to kraft paper or a layer of similar material. The brims did not appear to be quilted. The crowns were full, with the fullness created by a few wide tailored pleats. The tails of these bonnets were almost shoulder-length. Long ties were left undone so the sunbonnets flapped with a looseness similar in feel to that of the clothes with which they were shown: fluid shirts and pants, shorts with puffed legs, and blouses with puffed shoulders. Called the "Victory Garden" collection, the line appears to have been inspired by the years of the World Wars, and the hardworking spirit of the women of those eras, but also addresses contemporary concerns about sun exposure.

In the twenty-first century, we are only too aware of the aging effects of UV rays, the dangerous hole in the ozone (particularly of concern for those from the Southern Hemisphere, such as designer Karen Walker), and the high incidence of skin cancer. Why not revive the practical sunbonnet form? I have even seen young men in New York City sporting a type of baseball cap–shaped hat, which also utilizes a bavolet-type neck covering: a male, urban sunbonnet. The sunbonnet protects face, hair, and neck from sun damage, and the do-it-yourself aspect of its construction allows a wide scope for self-expression. Leopard print with shocking pink brim lining? Crisp solid white with a tailored tail? Slat-style with an abstract print? You decide.

There are many stories in the history of the American sunbonnet that are still waiting to be told but that were beyond the scope of this book. For instance, the history of women wearing sunbonnets in certain religious traditions, such as the Society of

Friends, deserves fuller treatment by a fashion historian.[18] This book focuses on the sunbonnet in Texas, but there are many other regions of the United States where the sunbonnet still awaits careful study. With each passing year, as American society moves further away from its agrarian heritage, the potential narrators for oral histories of the sunbonnet become fewer. These remaining voices should be recorded as quickly as possible.

The sunbonnet can be made from just a few scraps of calico, a little starch or cardboard, and a bit of thread; but embedded in this economical and deceptively simple construction is a portrait of the wearer, a confluence of practical function with her ideals of the beautiful, individual expression within the context of her heritage, and the history of American dress (Fig. 24).

Fig. 24. This gingham slat sunbonnet was probably made to match the dress. Dorothea Lange, "Mother and child of flood refugee family, near Memphis, Texas," May 1937, *Library of Congress, Prints and Photographs Division, FSA-OWI Collection, LC-USF34-016915-E (b&w film nitrate neg.).*

10

The Oral Histories

In this chapter, you will find the transcripts of the four main oral history interviews I conducted in 2004; these transcripts are reproduced here in their entirety (with a few exceptions, noted with asterisks where the interview went off on tangents not pertaining to sunbonnets, or with the word "indistinguishable" where I could not understand what was being said when listening to and transcribing the tapes later). The original tapes and transcripts of these interviews are housed in the Fashion Institute of Technology's Gladys Marcus Library Special Collections in New York City. However, I believe it is important to include the full text in this book, as well. First, I want to make this primary source information widely available to interested scholars and individuals. And second, I think the general reader can glean a better sense of the individual personalities involved by reading the transcripts as a whole.

Julia Brazil

Julia Brazil was born in Carmona, Polk County, Texas, on March 26, 1921, making her the youngest of the women participating in the taped interviews; she passed away on January 31, 2009. Julia spent her childhood in sawmill communities of Angelina and Nacogdoches counties, Texas. As a young woman, Julia worked as a telephone operator until her marriage to Charles Brazil on October 10, 1943. Julia lived in the Angelina County community of Redland for most of her adult life. Julia said that she viewed herself primarily as homemaker, wife, and mother, and felt that her children were her greatest accomplishment. This interview was conducted on April 7, 2004, in Lufkin, Texas.

> RJM: Rebecca Jumper Matheson, interviewer
> JB: Julia Brazil, narrator
> DRJ: Dana Rusk Jumper, observer

DRJ: And anytime you want to have her turn it off, or whatever, tell her because, like yesterday a couple of times, Faye had her turn it off because she wanted to say something else and she didn't want it recorded.

RJM: So you do wear sunbonnets, or when you were little you did?

JB: Oh, yeah.

RJM: When did you wear sunbonnets?

JB: Mostly when I was outside, because of the sun.

RJM: Did you work outside?

JB: I did when I'd clean my yard.

RJM: Did your family live in the country when you were growing up, or did they live in town?

JB: Well, it was mostly the country.

RJM: Where did you live when you were growing up?

JB: My daddy worked at the sawmill, and we'd move when he moved to another sawmill. 'Course, a lot of them are done away with now, you know. I lived at one called White City and another one in Nacogdoches [County]. Frost Johnson.

RJM: So, he worked in the mill, and did you live somewhere around the mill, then?

JB: We lived in a mill house, yeah.

RJM: So, did you have a garden around the mill houses, or—how were they set up? Were they right next to each other?

JB: They were right next to each other.

RJM: Did you grow vegetables or anything?

JB: [indistinguishable]

RJM: So did you wear a sunbonnet when you were out working in the garden?

JB: Yes. And most of the time I was out.

RJM: And, um, did you ever wear a bonnet when you went to church?

JB: No. [laughs]

RJM: What would you wear when you went to church?

JB: Well, back then we'd wear a hat. Not a big ol' hat, but just a small hat. Then it got to where most everyone went without anything.

RJM: When you did wear a sunbonnet, what type—or, how was it made in the front? There's two different kinds.

JB: Mama made these, it went over your face, and then they starched that real stiff, and then on the back, they'd sew a piece of material come down on your neck you know, and I guess it would be longer than the one come over your head because it gathered and had a drawstring, and then they'd pull that drawstring up to pull it together . . . and of course it had a tie. But it would come over your face real stiff. It seems like, but I may be wrong, that they used to stitch in it.

RJM: Did your mom do any designs in the stitching or did she just do it straight across?

JB: She'd just do it straight across. There had to be something in there, you know, to stiffen it.

RJM: What did she put in there, do you know?

JB: Probably two pieces, two pieces of material together.
[Bell rings. "Hello"—sounds of nurse attending to JB's next-door neighbor.]

RJM: Do you remember any of the ones that had, like, cardboard staves in them?

JB: I've seen them, but it don't seem like she used them in hers. But she could've put them in that top. I have seen them.

RJM: What kind of fabric did she usually make the bonnets from?

JB: Just cotton.

RJM: And where did she get the fabric from?

JB: Mostly—they called it the commissary—it was the store at the mill. We'd get our material and everything.

RJM: And would she go in and buy fabric just for the bonnets, or would she buy everything at the same time?

JB: I imagine everything at the same time, as probably our clothes.

RJM: Did you ever have a bonnet to match any of your dresses?

JB: Do what?

RJM: Did you ever have a bonnet that matched any of your dresses?

JB: I don't remember that.

RJM: Did you ever see a bonnet that was made out of fancier materials, or did you ever have one?

JB: Mostly what I saw was made out of cotton.

RJM: Do you remember any made out of designs?

JB: You mean, the material?

RJM: Yes.

JB: Some of them were just solid; they might have been out of designs, but I don't remember that.

RJM: So when you went to buy something at the commissary at the mill, did you pay cash, or did you have credit?

JB: No, you get a check [Author's note: these tokens were more commonly known as chits].

RJM: So you'd get paid in a check—

JB: It kind of looked like little money. They were bigger than a penny—I can't describe it, now. It wasn't a check like, you know, paper. It was really a coin, I guess.

RJM: And then you'd be able to spend that.

JB: Uh-huh, yeah. I think that's what they paid them in wages.

RJM: So did she sew those by hand, or do you know, did she use a machine?

JB: She had a treadle machine.

RJM: And did she use a pattern?

JB: She probably did to cut it out.

RJM: Did you ever learn to make patterns or anything?

JB: No, I never did.

RJM: Did your mom teach you how to sew?

JB: Well, some.

RJM: Did you wear a bonnet when you went to school?

JB: No.

RJM: Did you wear a hat, or did you go bareheaded?

JB: We'd go bareheaded.

RJM: When you were, or if you were outside and you put a bonnet on, what was the main reason you would wear one?

JB: Mostly to keep the sun off.

RJM: Did you like wearing a bonnet, or did your mom make you?

JB: Well—they were hot. [laughter]

RJM: What made it hot?

JB: Well, that coming down on your neck. They're hot.

RJM: Why did you want to keep the sun off?

JB: Well, to keep from blistering.

RJM: Well, let's see, did you have any sisters in your family?

JB: I had two.

RJM: Did they wear bonnets also?

JB: I'm sure they did.

RJM: Were they older or younger than you?

JB: They were older. I was the youngest.

RJM: This part of the bonnet—do you have a name for the part of the bonnet that comes out over your face?

JB: I don't know what they would call that. I just remember that it was stiff. And what I was telling you about, was gathered there in the back, would make it come up higher over your head—look fuller there.

RJM: OK. And what about the part that came down the back of your neck, how long was that?

JB: It was about down to here, about down to—it didn't come down on your shoulder, it was just to protect your neck.

RJM: And would your clothes come up about that high? Would it meet your collar?

JB: Yeah.

RJM: Did you have a name for that part, that's down on your neck?

JB: I don't know what they called that. I know it was to protect your neck.

DRJ: I just had something come to mind, a question—um, you know Mother used to I guess make the bonnets.

JB: Mm-hmm.

DRJ: Was there ever a place where you could actually go out and buy them? Or did everyone just make their own?

JB: Probably way back there, there wasn't. Now, I know that recently, it wasn't too long ago, when we had those bazaars at church, Mrs. O'Neal, she made some real pretty ones and sold them.

DRJ: Right. There was so much work in them.

JB: Mm-hmm. And she would make them and give them to people she knew, you know. I think she gave me one, and I can't think what I did with it. I guess it's at home somewhere. I wish I could have got out there and found it.

DRJ: Yes.

JB: I can't get nowhere.

DRJ: Did you all launder your bonnets yourselves? Did you wash it and starch it? Was each person responsible for doing her own bonnet?

JB: Probably was. You know, back then you had to do it with your arms, you know. There wasn't no electric. I guess you could buy starch, way back then.

RJM: So do you remember starching your bonnets yourself?

JB: [indistinguishable]

RJM: How old were you when you stopped wearing bonnets? Did you stop?

JB: Oh, I had one at home. And I was working in my yard there at home. It's been a good while, but it wasn't way back.

RJM: So would you still pick a bonnet? If you were going to get outside this afternoon, would you rather have a bonnet or a hat?

JB: I think I'd rather have a bonnet because a hat mashes your hair.

RJM: So it was easier to keep your hair done under a bonnet?

JB: Yes, because it doesn't mash it down. Like I used to wear my hair with curls all on top—it isn't right now—but I would hate for it to get all mashed down. And it's good being up off of your face. A hat just mashes your hair all down.

RJM: I guess that's because the bonnet comes up high in the back?

JB: Yes, it comes up high in the back, makes the bonnet come up high off your face. Made them pretty.

RJM: So you basically kept wearing the bonnet for outdoor work.

JB: Yeah, I did. Because Mama kept making them as long as she lived.

DRJ: Did your mother wear them to church, or just to work in?

JB: No, just to work in.

DRJ: Well, I remember Mrs. Bowers, the old Mrs. Bowers, that lived down the road from us. And she had a Sunday bonnet. It was a black bonnet. It was a dress bonnet, and she would show that to the kids.

JB: Did she wear it to church?

DRJ: Well, I assume that she did, because she told us. She was not able to get around very much at that time. But I'm assuming she did because she told us it was her Sunday bonnet.

JB: I don't remember seeing her wearing it or not. I might have, and forgot it.

DRJ: Well, Mother always seemed to prefer her bonnet, and she wore it until just a couple of years ago, when she was able to get out. She wears a bonnet.

JB: Did she make hers?

DRJ: Or people would give her ones that they had made.

JB: Mm-hmm.

DRJ: Are those all your questions?

RJM: I think so.

DRJ: I think it's so interesting.

JB: Never would have thought anybody would care about a bonnet. I knew the old people—most all the old people did wear them.

RJM: Can I ask you what year you were born?

JB: The third, twenty-sixth, twenty-one.

RJM: Thank you, that helps me date everything, too.

JB: Oh, well, good luck. I wish I could have remembered the names of things.

RJM: Oh, no, no, that's good.

Lillie Faye McLain Rusk

Faye Rusk was born on March 20, 1914, in Nacogdoches County, Texas, and spent her childhood there. She and her husband, Ellis Rusk, were married for sixty-two years before he passed away. A loquacious storyteller, Faye had a vibrant personality and an enthusiasm for life. This interview was conducted on April 6, 2004, in Nacogdoches, Texas; Faye died on December 29, 2004, in Houston, Texas.

RJM: Rebecca Jumper Matheson, interviewer

FMR: Faye McLain Rusk, narrator

DRJ: Dana Rusk Jumper, observer

FMR: I was ninety the 20th of March.

RJM: Congratulations! Happy birthday. So whenever you went outside, your mother told you to put your sunbonnet on.

FMR: Yes. They were very hot. You know how bonnets are made . . . under here they tie. . . . We lived in a house that had a hallway and it had doors and whenever you'd close those doors, it would slam and Mama would say, "Close those doors when you go out, and get that bonnet!" [general laughter] She always said that.

RJM: Where did you keep your bonnets? Outside somewhere?

FMR: Under the hat rack. There was a bonnet rack right under the men's hat rack, where children couldn't reach them.

RJM: On the porch, or was that inside the house?

FMR: It was in the hallway to the house.

RJM: Now, what kind of bonnets did you wear? I've seen a couple of different styles.

FMR: Some of them had wider brims, and it was quilted. Mama sometimes would quilt. . . .

There were Sunday bonnets and everyday bonnets. When I was born and raised, in the country, we were outside a whole lot. And my mother had beautiful skin, and she said, "You're going to ruin your skin. And you won't be able to go out in the world from being out in the sunbeams too much."

RJM: And you wore the bonnet so you wouldn't?

FMR: Wouldn't suntan. And now, I have a daughter—she takes everything she can off and goes into the backyard and gets all the sun she can!

RJM: Well, that's how things—

FMR: Things change.

RJM: Whether you want it to be fair or darker changes.

FMR: Bonnets were made . . . they came over with the pilgrims. You'll have to do a little more research on that. And the men wore the pointy hats.

RJM: Now, with the bonnets you wore, what were they usually made of?

FMR: Some sort of cotton or taffeta material. Some of gingham. Dark colors for winter, light colors for summer. And my grandmother had a black bonnet. She wore it to church, she wore it everywhere she went. She had one that she sat there on the porch in the afternoon in. She didn't want the wind to get on her face.

RJM: Now, the cotton I'm guessing would be, like, an everyday bonnet, the taffeta for dress?

FMR: Yes. In the winter you'd wear dark colors. My mother always had a black bonnet, and my grandmother, but that wouldn't be what the children would use.

RJM: What color would the children wear?

FMR: Just about the same material, floral prints and check—gingham—they had to be washed and starched. They'd be starched real stiff, and then you ironed it.

RJM: Did you do the cold water starch? Or another method?

FMR: Cold water starch. Did you ever do one up?

RJM: I haven't done one myself.

FMR: I tell you, they're hard to do. Some of them have a crown that sticks up and is pulled into a little circle there.

RJM: Did you ever wear one of the kind that has the staves in it?

FMR: No, I didn't, but I know my grandmother had those. . . . I have one [a bonnet] out at the house.

RJM: Oh, do you really? I'd love to see it at some point, if you had a chance. I'd love to see what it looks like. Is it one of the quilted brim type?

FMR: Yes. Blue print. I kept it; I quit wearing it, but I kept it all these years. I kept it, though it had gone out of style; it was still serviceable. I have put it on and worked out in the yard some. But they sure are hot!

[General laughter]

RJM: Well, when did you stop wearing your bonnet?

FMR: When did I stop? Well . . . it probably would have been twenty years . . . maybe when I was sixty?

RJM: So you kept wearing them—well, you wore them when you were growing up, and when you were an adult you wore them also, then?

FMR: Yes, if I was outside. [Indistinguishable] You know how they used to have a cemetery working? Well, I had gone over to Rock Springs—

RJM: That's where I got married!

FMR: Oh, it is?

RJM: Yes!

FMR: Well, my mother's mother and daddy were buried over there, and we'd always go over there. . . . There was a regular reunion, and we'd work that cemetery. So I saw a girl I knew, Juanita Birch, and she had on a straw hat. They had moved to Houston. So I asked her, "Where did you get that hat?" And she told me where she had bought it in Houston, and that it was seventy-five cents. So I said to my grandma and grandpa when I got home . . . I said, "Grandpa, I want to work for you. I want to make seventy-five cents, because I want a straw hat."

And he said, "Yeah, OK, I'll let you work for me." He was chewing tobacco. He used to tease me. And I'd start running around that house and he'd start running around chasing me. But anyway, he knew I wanted this straw hat. And we had what was called the hog pasture. And it was fenced in.

And he said, "OK, if you cut bitter weeds." That was an old weed, that yellow weed, that was thick as hops up there. "If you cut the bitter weeds out of that hog pasture, I'll give you seventy-five cents." Grandma was sitting there.

She said, "Walt!" (His name was Walter, they called him Walt.) She said, "Walt! Walt! That child can't do that!" He'd just tease the heck out of us.

So I said, "OK, you just get me a hoe and I'll do it." So he sharpened a hoe and I got out there—and it was summertime— it was as hot as the dickens! So I hoed all day. Then I got up bright and early as the daylight. And my grandmother cooked ham. She always cooked ham, because I loved ham so well. She made ham and biscuits. I went up there the next morning, and I got that hoe again and I chopped weeds.

RJM: Now, were you wearing a sunbonnet while you were doing all this?

FMR: Yes. Yes, I was.

And I said, "Grandpa, did you mean the *whole* thing?"

He said, "Yes, that's what you said."

I said, "No, that's what you said. I told you that I would, that I would try." So I went back out there after lunch. And I got so hot, my grandma came to the end of the porch—they had a beautiful country home—and she said, "Faye, come on in here and rest a while." And I came on in and she had Grandpa sitting down, and she had me sitting down by him, and she said, "Now, Walt, that child has cut enough; she's cut more than seventy-five cents worth." [General laughter] "Just cut it off right now and give her her money. She's going to have a heat stroke."

And he said, "Well, I won't."

And she said, "Well, I will. She went to go get her purse and give me seventy-five cents, and Grandpa got out his money and gave me seventy-five cents!"

[General laughter]

RJM: And did you get your hat?

FMR: Yes, I got my straw hat. My mama said when I bought it, "Don't you know you're going to have that worn out before next year?" She was the only one that had a straw hat. And I said, "Well, I'll save mine." So I wore it part-time, just for very special.

RJM: And you'd wear your bonnet the rest of the time.

FMR: Mm-hmm.

[Indistinguishable]

RJM: So why did you like that straw hat so much better than the sunbonnet?

FMR: Cooler—it was much cooler. It had a wide brim. Those bonnets are hot! You pull those down on both sides—you don't get much air in the front.

RJM: So did it still keep the sun off of you pretty well?

FMR: Yes.

RJM: What about the back of your neck?

FMR: Well, it was wide-brimmed.

RJM: So did your sunbonnets usually have the part in the back that comes down?

FMR: Yes—the tail.

RJM: And how long was the tail on your bonnets?

FMR: It was to your shoulders, where you wouldn't get sunburned. You wore it to the fields to pick cotton, chop cotton, anything like that. Out in the hot sun. They'd protect you all right. But they were miserable!

[General laughter]

RJM: So, have you ever made a sunbonnet?

FMR: No.

RJM: Who made the sunbonnets for your family?

FMR: My mother.

RJM: Your mother made them. What did she use to make them? Did she buy new fabric, or did she reuse?

FMR: No, we'd head to town. And you'd pick out what fabric you wanted for your bonnet. And you'd usually have a dress and a bonnet, matching.

RJM: So did you ever wear a bonnet to church?

FMR: No.

RJM: What would you wear when you went to church?

FMR: We had Sunday hats. My older sisters might have, but I didn't.

RJM: So would the hat have been more fashionable than the bonnet?

FMR: Yes!

RJM: Did anybody around you wear bonnets to church?

FMR: Yes. A lot of people did, that couldn't afford a hat. They'd make the bonnets out of some material. People utilized everything they had. I can remember, I didn't have to have it, but during the Depression, people would make things out of food or flour sacks—it was just like a print, like a bolt of material. Kids would come to school wearing it, and I'd recognize the flour sacks. And I knew they were, because we had bought the same flour! [General laughter] We never did wear the flour sack dresses.

RJM: So tell me about the ones that people—do you know anything else about the ones that have the staves in them? Did anybody in your family wear those?

FMR: Oh yes. The staves were like the flat part of a fan. I don't know where they came from. My grandmother had one. And she always had the black bonnet she wore to church.

They'd take their fingers and just open up all the little ruffles. She'd redo that ruffle with the lace.

RJM: And that was with starch?

FMR: Yes.

RJM: So, she'd basically pleat it again?

FMR: Yes.

RJM: Did you ever watch her starch them?

FMR: Yes—I've done it.

RJM: You've starched them. Well, tell me about the starching process.

FMR: Well, you'd get your starch ready. Get it wet. I'd let it lay a while. And then you'd iron it. The iron wasn't electric. You'd put it in the fire.

★   ★   ★

RJM: Now how would they actually do the pleats? Now, would that happen while it was cold?

FMR: It would be lifting it upwards and out. If you were to just iron, you'd just be going round and round and round. She'd open them up with her fingers. That was just for our Sunday bonnets. That wasn't for the ones we'd wear to the field.

RJM: Right. So what did you do to care for the ones you wore, like, just in the field? Did you wash those?

FMR: Oh yes, washed and boiled. They were in perspiration every day.

RJM: How often did they get washed?

FMR: Once a week. I always liked washing, because you didn't have to go to the field. It took all of us to wash.

RJM: So did you starch your field bonnets?

FMR: Yes, they were starched.

RJM: Did you iron those as well?

FMR: Yes, they were ironed as well. I've seen some real beautiful bonnets. . . . I remember Miss Annie Millard—you all know Millard's Crossing?—you know where that is? Miss Annie and Jesse Millard—They went to Old North Church, that's where I go to church. She always had a white bonnet, and a white dress. I can just see her coming in with that white dress on and that white bonnet, just starched.

RJM: Going back to bonnets, how did you wear your hair underneath the bonnet? Did you pull it back in any way?

FMR: We just left it down. You got your hair wet [with perspiration] every day, so you washed it every night.

RJM: So, tell me about the names for the different parts of the bonnet. This is the tail in the back, and

FMR: Crown—and

RJM: What about the part that sticks out around your face?

FMR: Brim. That's the brim.

RJM: So the main thing was protecting your skin.

FMR: And hair.

RJM: What would happen if the sun was on your hair?

FMR: It would bleach it.

RJM: And you didn't want that, either?

FMR: No. . . . You can tell when someone's been out without anything on their head. And everybody wore them. You didn't look different than anyone else; everyone wore bonnets.

RJM: So what made the bonnets nicer—what would make one bonnet nicer than another?

FMR: Materials—and the seamstress! Mama would make designs on ours.

RJM: In the quilting?

FMR: Yes.

RJM: Oh! Well, tell me about some of those. What different designs did she do? What shapes?

FMR: Sometimes she'd make stars. Or cut a picture out of a paper or catalog—of a doll maybe—and trace it on there and stitch it. We didn't have polyester then. It was cotton in the brim, to make the brim stiff.

RJM: So was there anything else in there besides the cotton? There's two layers of fabric and the cotton in the middle.

FMR: Well, some of them didn't have any cotton. Some of them had the, what do you call it, when you make a quilt?

RJM: Batting?

FMR: Batting.

RJM: So did they buy the batting new?

FMR: Mama would card the cotton. Have you ever seen cards?

RJM: Yes.

DRJ: I think I have.

FMR: It would straighten the cotton out, where it was smooth.

RJM: So you'd card your own cotton, and use that—

FMR: In the brim. When you washed it, it had to be done just right, or the cotton would pack down, or knot up.

RJM: And in the back of yours, did you have anything to tighten it up in the back?

FMR: We had the drawstring. What made the best, Mama always said, was a shoestring, a man's shoestring, Oxford type. So it wouldn't unravel.

RJM: Yes, I know, because some of them ravel a lot. On the streamers on the front, were those usually finished off on the edges, or were those just left?

FMR: They were hemmed.

RJM: They were hemmed.

★　★　★

RJM: Did you have anything to make the crown stick up?

FMR: Just the starch.

RJM: Just the starching it.

DRJ: Did you always use the same pattern?

FMR: Mama had one she liked; there were many kinds.

DRJ: But basically the ones you wore were all the same style?

FMR: Yes.

163

DRJ: Once you found something you liked you stayed with it.

FMR: I bet you Louise [Ed. note: Louise Jenkins Rusk, interview following] has a bonnet right now.

DRJ: Oh she does! And she would still be wearing them outside to work in if she were able to get out. She's always worn her bonnet.

FMR: My mother did, too.

★ ★ ★

RJM: So were your hairdos a lot flatter then?

FMR: Oh yes, we didn't have a permanent.

RJM: So it was pretty natural.

FMR: Yes. It was just if you had curly hair naturally.

RJM: So curly hair was pretty popular then?

FMR: Yes. If you had curly hair natural it was special. It [hair] was hard to deal with.

DRJ: Especially when you're working outside every day.

FMR: You washed it every day. And when you wash it so much it would get so dry.

RJM: How long did you have your hair at that time?

FMR: I had it about like yours. Just above the shoulders. I had bangs.

RJM: So—a bob?

FMR: Yes.

★   ★   ★

FMR: I was thirteen years old when I had a permanent. I thought I was in high cotton! They didn't even have a beauty shop in Nacogdoches. I had an aunt—she wanted a permanent. It cost two dollars from a traveling salesman. He rented a room in a house. And we went down there, and we got our permanent. Then it started to grow out and we had curls down here, and flat up here! But we thought it was pretty. We weren't the only ones either.

Louise Jenkins Rusk

My grandmother, Louise Jenkins Rusk (Fig. 11), was born on September 23, 1912, and spent her childhood in Nacogdoches County, Texas. She was not given a middle name, which was unusual for that place and time. Her earliest memory was of seeing her mother's dead body laid out in the parlor; Louise was just three years old when her mother passed away. She grew up the indulged youngest sibling in a farming family of five children. She loved to cook for the praise it garnered from others; she loved to garden for herself; but she valued duty and hard work and rarely admitted to doing anything just for fun. Nevertheless, my younger sister and I have childhood memories of a Louise who was playful while she was in her seventies: delighting in spraying us with the water hose while watering her flower garden, teasing us with the imaginary "Tippy" flying insect (which I always imagined as a dirt dauber), making playhouses of pine straw with us, and teaching us to make corn cob dolls. She loved clothes, yet when she died she left boxes of unworn garments she was saving for "best." Her decorating style was to display every gift she had ever received, but the inside of her house was never really her home: her true habitat was her garden. This interview took place on April 9, 2004, at her house in the Redland community outside Lufkin, Angelina County, Texas. Louise died on June 15, 2008, at the age of ninety-five.

LJR: Louise Jenkins Rusk
RJM: Rebecca Jumper Matheson

RJM: OK, so, tell me about when you wore bonnets growing up. When did you wear them? What kind of activities were you doing?

LJR: Well, we had to work in the fields, you know. Chop cotton first, and then pick it later after it matured and got ready to pick; and we had to chop cotton.

RJM: And what does that involve? What do you do when you chop cotton?

LJR: Well, they plant it pretty thick in a row, and of course we have to cut out some of it and get the grass out by hoeing it.

RJM: Like weeding it and thinning it out.

LJR: Like weeding it, you could say, and thinning it, yes. The corn that we would thin would have to be left—oh, about a foot or a foot and a half apart, a stalk. Now, am I going too fast?

RJM: Oh, you're fine. So, you'd wear them when you worked outside then?

LJR: Uh-huh. I guess I started wearing them when I was about fourteen—somewhere along—earlier than that really.

RJM: When you were a little girl did you wear them?

LJR: I'm not sure. I know I remember my Grandmother Lankford wearing them.

RJM: When she was working outside?

LJR: Uh-huh. And she had a little black taffeta bonnet for her dress wear, well as I remember.

RJM: And what did it look like? Can you describe it a little bit?

LJR: Well, it had a small brim. It was fancier than the ones we worked in the field in. And she wore those for dress wear.

RJM: Did it have any decoration on it?

LJR: No, just some strings to tie. Now some of them could have had little ruffles around them, I guess they did. But well as I remember hers, it was just plain. Black taffeta, I think, is what it was made from.

RJM: Would that have had a quilted type brim?

LJR: Mm-hmm. Just a little smaller one than the ones we worked in.

RJM: OK.

LJR: Little bit dressy.

RJM: So the dressier ones didn't come quite so far out.

LJR: No.

RJM: Is that because you wouldn't have been outside for as long in those?

LJR: Yes. And I think some of them had little ruffles for decoration around this brim.

RJM: So, when you were a little girl, then, it wasn't as important to wear a bonnet when you were outside?

LJR: No.

RJM: But when you got to be a teenager it was more important?

LJR: Mm-hmm.

RJM: So why was that? Why was it more important as you got to be a teenager?

LJR: Well, you wanted to take care of your complexion better. You wanted to look better by that time. Started growing up, you know.

RJM: [Laughs] Oh, OK. So it was sort of part of being ladylike?

LJR: Uh-huh. I guess that's what you would call it.

RJM: So did anybody—or, who told you that you needed to take care of your complexion?

LJR: I guess my grandmother. Or my older sisters, probably, by that time. I was small when we left my grandmother. About—I guess I was around six or seven, something like that, when we moved from Mt. Enterprise to Pisgah.

RJM: So tell me a little bit about the bonnets you wore out in the field. What did they look like?

LJR: Oh, we had some with staves in them. I've told you about that before, or have I?

RJM: Describe—go ahead and tell me about it again.

LJR: Well, it would be a wide brim, come out to protect us from the sun. And we would make—we'd sew in strips down that brim. And cut out pasteboard staves, we called them, to slip in those slots. It would hold it up out of our face. It didn't have to be starched, see.

RJM: About how wide were each one of the staves?

LJR: I'd say about an inch and a half. Cut them out of pasteboard. And they'd slip in those slots and hold it up off of our face. That was our work bonnets.

RJM: Right. And what would you do when you washed the bonnet then?

LJR: Take the staves out.

RJM: But you were saying you didn't have to starch it?

LJR: They would hold it in place, off of our face, see. And they were not as much work, [compared] to ironing them.

RJM: Did you still have to iron them anyway?

LJR: We didn't to work in. Those staves would hold them up off of our face.

RJM: How deep was it? How far off of your face did it come?

LJR: Let's see. They were pretty long. I would say about six or eight inches wide. I'm guessing.

RJM: Yeah.

LJR: Is this recording everything?

RJM: Yes.

LJR: Tell me if I'm saying the wrong thing.

RJM: You won't say anything wrong! [Both laugh] Um, let's see. So, um, how often did you actually wash them? How often did you do the laundry?

LJR: Well, as often as we did the other laundry. Back then, if we did a laundry once a week, we did well. You know, it was a task to draw your water and boil them in a wash pot. So we usually just washed a big washing back then.

RJM: So did everybody help out in that, or was that somebody's job specifically?

LJR: Well, that was the women's job. The girls and women. In our case, when we moved out to ourselves, it was just my daddy and us children. And I was the youngest of the five, you know. We really had it rough.

RJM: So, um, what about—did you have any—did you have any dress bonnets? Or did you just have field bonnets?

LJR: As well as I remember, we just had the work bonnets.

RJM: And what did you wear when you dressed up? Did you wear any kind of headcovering when you dressed up?

LJR: We had hats part of the time.

RJM: So, when you were growing up, who made your bonnets for you?

LJR: Well, my sister Leila was the main seamstress in our family, so I'm sure she did it. I can't remember for sure. But I know in later years she did the sewing for us.

RJM: Right.

LJR: And she made me some—I thought—real cute things then. Without a pattern even! Just look at a picture or tell her how we wanted it, you know. She'd make it the best she could—and we wore them, anyway!

RJM: Did she just draw up her own patterns, or did she just cut away?

LJR: She'd have patterns to some things. Some, she made her own.

RJM: What did she use to make patterns out of?

LJR: Just newspaper.

RJM: So when you were outside in the fields, tell me about your outfit. Tell me what you would wear on a typical day, going out to work in the cotton fields.

LJR: Just our common, everyday clothes. Which looked pretty bad—some of them.

RJM: What would that be? Besides a bonnet—did you always wear a bonnet?

LJR: Not too much. I didn't take care of myself till I got to be a teenager. [Laughter] I'd go out bareheaded and bare-armed, and just get blistered and everything part of the time, you know. 'Course, being dark, I didn't blister like Sudie, my sister, or Leila. They were light complected. And Jessie, my oldest sister, and my brother and I were dark complected.

RJM: Right.

LJR: My daddy was fair, and my mother was dark complected. So, some took after one and some the other.

RJM: So it seems that it would have been an advantage, then, to have a darker complexion if it didn't burn.

LJR: Didn't blister like they did.

RJM: But when you got older, you decided that you needed to cover up more?

LJR: Uh-huh. Decided I'd better look a little better.

RJM: So to look better, you had to—

LJR: Wear bonnets, and long sleeves. Kind of take care of myself a little better.

RJM: So you'd wear long sleeves, then, when you worked outside.

LJR: Mm-hmm.

RJM: So, would that be, like, a long-sleeved shirt, or a dress—what would you normally wear?

LJR: Yes, I wore a dress until I got up older—and I wore overalls some.

RJM: Tell me about your overalls.

LJR: [laughs] They were striped.

RJM: What color stripes?

LJR: Blue and white. Real dark blue, and the stripes were just about that wide.

RJM: About a half an inch?

LJR: Not a half. About a fourth, I guess, of an inch.

RJM: What kind of fabric was it?

LJR: Cotton.

RJM: Cotton. Was that something Leila sewed?

LJR: No, she didn't make those. They were bought, ready-made.

RJM: So where would you buy something like that in Nacogdoches? Did you order it, or did you go into a store?

LJR: I don't remember ordering them. I suppose we bought them in Nacogdoches. I can't remember about that.

RJM: Did you all ever go into town to shop, or did your dad mostly do the shopping?

LJR: We did go, occasionally. Then, later, we had friends that had cars that would take us. We did have a buggy that was a little bit better than a wagon, to travel in. But we didn't own any cars.

RJM: So do you remember ever going in to buy fabric for anything? For any of your clothes, did you ever get to go pick out fabric, or did somebody else pick it out?

LJR: I suppose my sisters did that. Leila, especially. Because I don't remember buying it myself. So I guess she did it.

RJM: So what kind of, um, fabric did they make out of—did they actually go buy fabric for a bonnet? Did they just use what was left over, or did they cut up old things to make a bonnet?

LJR: Some of them. The ones we worked in were made out of old clothes. We didn't go buy new material for that. We just used what we had, you know. So old clothes, of any kind.

RJM: So it was almost like a way to reuse that fabric again. If you had an old dress, would you maybe, like, cut it up when it wore out, is that what you're—

LJR: Uh-huh. Had to make it out of pretty good material or it wouldn't last long.

RJM: So what were sort of the different designs on a bonnet?

LJR: Some of them were checks. Some just solid colors. Just anything we had for the old work bonnets.

RJM: So did your neighbors wear bonnets as well? Other people in the area?

LJR: Did they do what?

RJM: Did they also wear sunbonnets?

LJR: Um-hum. To work in, yes, they did.

RJM: So how comfortable is it to wear a bonnet?

LJR: Well, it's comfortable if you don't tie them too tight. You know they have strings on them to tie. And if you don't tie them too tight, they're comfortable. Don't bother you at all. You know Eileen [Ed. note: narrator Eileen Johnson] makes all kinds of bonnets.

[Indistinguishable]

RJM: Showed me one of hers with the staves in it. [Discussing interview with Minnie Lee Skelton, following]

LJR: Well, that was good!

RJM: Yes, it was good. She said it was probably from the 1920s. So it's neat to see those. And I've gotten to look at your poke-type one, the one with the quilted brim.

LJR: Yes.

RJM: Now you started wearing those later on, right? The ones with the quilted brims rather than the staves?

LJR: The ones with the staves were the first work bonnets that I can remember. Then later we started wearing them with the narrow brim. Like the one I gave you.

RJM: Right. Like the one you have now. And did you make some of those through the years? Did you make ever—either kind?

LJR: I suppose I did, but I can't remember for sure. I imagine I did. Had to do so many things, not having a mother, you know. Sure makes a difference.

RJM: Now, what about when you were grown up? By the time you got married, for example, what kind of bonnet were you wearing then, as a young married woman?

LJR: Like the one I gave you.

RJM: With the quilted type brim.

LJR: Uh-huh. Just to work in. I never did care for a hat. Lot of women wore hats out working. But I preferred my bonnet.

RJM: And what did you find made a bonnet better to work in?

LJR: Just some kind of printed cotton material.

RJM: Um, what was it about a bonnet that was better than a hat, for example?

LJR: For one thing, I could keep them on better. The hat was inclined to come loose and blow off of my head.

RJM: So having it tied on securely was a good thing.

LJR: Um-hmm. I think I threw away the last old straw hat I had hanging back there. But I have one bonnet left.

RJM: Yes. But you did wear a straw hat sometimes, too?

LJR: Sometimes I did wear a hat to work in.

RJM: Now how did the hat keep the sun off of you, compared to a bonnet? Did it do as good a job on that?

LJR: Yes, if it had a wide brim, it would do just as good as a bonnet. And lots of women preferred the hats, rather than the bonnets.

RJM: Why did they like hats better? Do you know?

LJR: I don't know unless it stayed up off of their face better; the bonnet comes down closer to your face. And the hat, with the brim out, stays away from your face better.

RJM: So you can see a little better, is that it?

LJR: Yes, you can. And, too, some of them were so wide that they'd shade your face better than the narrow brim bonnets.

RJM: Now, when you were a young married woman, I know you moved out to West Texas for a while. What did the women wear for working out there?

LJR: Some of them wore bonnets, some hats. The wind blew so much out there, it was hard to keep anything on your head!

RJM: Even a bonnet? That was hard to keep on, too?

LJR: Yes! It did blow hard out there sometimes. Had sand storms, like you'd wake up in the morning and it'd be so pretty and still and look like it was going to be a beautiful day, and maybe you'd start to washing and the first thing you knew, sand was all in the air. Out there it did.

RJM: That must have been hard.

LJR: It was. Especially when you had to use the wash pot, and hang them on the line. Oh! People have it so much easier these days.

RJM: Did anybody out in West Texas wear the kind with the staves in it, or did they wear the other kind of bonnet?

LJR: I can't remember seeing any of the kind with staves out there. They'd just have the wide brim and starch them stiff. And wore hats a lot.

RJM: Do you remember any of the ways the brims were quilted on the bonnets? Like, I've seen some that are just straight. And I've seen some of them that have designs.

LJR: Yes, some of them would have different designs. Going up and down like a fence row. I mean the old-timey rail fence rows. You know, zigzag-like across the brim. And just different cute designs that they liked.

RJM: So tell me a little bit about starching. About how you go about starching a bonnet. Say I've washed it. Now, how do I get that brim, if I've got the quilted type brim, how do I get that brim to stand out?

LJR: I use that—what's the name? Faultless starch. Cold starch they call it. Mix the amount of starch you want with water and just put that bonnet in there and wring it out. And then when it dried you would sprinkle it with water and iron it and that would make it real stiff where it would stand up off your face.

RJM: And did you do the whole thing or just part of it?

LJR: I did the whole thing, just starch it in cold starch it was called.

RJM: So tell me about the different names for the parts of the bonnet. We've already talked about the brim, the part up here, that sticks out over your face. What about the top?

LJR: Well, that's the crown. It's just plain, just plain cloth you know, cut by a pattern, then you sew the ties on underneath this brim.

RJM: And then I know a lot of them, you can sort of adjust in the back.

LJR: Yes, drawstring it's called. You sew a little place back there; you put a little piece of cloth across about that wide. Sew it kind of halfway down—as far as you want it—and put a drawstring in there so you can draw it up the way you want it to fit you the best.

RJM: What would you use to make the drawstring out of?

LJR: Just some of the material that the bonnet was made of.

RJM: And did you finish off the edges of that, or was it un-hemmed?

LJR: Far as I remember, it was just unhemmed. Just a string-like that you sewed over to the side, to hold it in place, and you'd put it through with a safety pin or something.

RJM: Now, what about the part of the bonnet that goes back over your neck?

LJR: That's part of the brim? Not the brim, the crown?

RJM: OK.

LJR: You know, this part that goes all the way back. The crown.

RJM: Now what about the tail? I've heard you use that term before.

LJR: Tail. Well, it's the bottom part of the bonnet from where the drawstring is on back. Am I making any sense to you?

RJM: You sure are. You're making lots of sense!

LJR: Oh dear. Sounds kind of ridiculous.

RJM: No, it doesn't! It doesn't sound ridiculous at all. Sounds great.

LJR: I was just thinking I did have an old bonnet that was your great-grandmother's, and I'm not sure whether I gave it to your mother or if it's still in the cedar chest.

RJM: Was it the green and white one?

LJR: Green and white check.

RJM: Mother's got that one.

LJR: Well, that's the one I had in mind. It was her grandmother's.

RJM: I've seen that one; that's a neat one.

LJR: Well, that's the one I was thinking about.

RJM: That's kind of a little one. It doesn't have a real deep brim, which I thought was interesting.

LJR: No.

RJM: Wouldn't be nearly as deep as the one with the staves on it.

LJR: Oh no. That was one they'd probably wear when they was just visiting around their neighbor or something. You know, a little bit dressier than the ones with the staves in. They were to work in, in the field.

RJM: So did you ever have a bonnet to go visiting in, or is that something that your grandmother's generation would have done?

LJR: That was in my grandmother's generation. We went bareheaded most of the time. Only when we'd really dress up we'd wear hats most of the time.

RJM: So do you remember your grandmother wearing bonnets a lot?

LJR: Seems like she wore them quite a bit when she went out. Probably wore them to church—her little black bonnet.

RJM: So when you came in, did you take your field bonnet off when you came into the house?

LJR: Mm-hmm.

RJM: Where did you put it then when you took it off?

LJR: Probably hung it up somewhere to have it for the next day.

RJM: Did you have a special place where you hung them, or put them up?

LJR: No. I imagine we just threw them down where we threw our work clothes.

RJM: So did you change out of your work clothes when you came in, also?

LJR: I think we did. Or we could have worn them till we took a bath to go to bed.

RJM: What about your hair underneath the bonnet? Did you have to pull it back to put the bonnet on, or did you just leave it?

LJR: Just kind of push it back a little to get the bonnet on, I guess. That's been a long time ago.

RJM: Do you remember anything about how you were wearing your hair, when you were a teenager?

LJR: Wore it kind of short most of the time.

RJM: Shorter than mine? [About one inch above shoulder.]

LJR: Little bit.

RJM: So you had one of those fashionable bobs!

LJR: When I was a little bitty thing, about three or four years old, I have a picture of Macre Walker and myself, and I had bangs.

RJM: I have a copy of that one! That one's really cute. [Laughter]

LJR: They said that when my mother lived, she curled my hair. I have a kind of natural wave anyway, and she would fix it in long curls. But I don't have a picture of it like that.

RJM: So if you were making the kind of bonnet with the quilted type brim, what would you put in it to stiffen it? Would you need anything besides the fabric to make it stiffer?

LJR: Yes, you'd starch a piece of any kind of cloth that you wanted to use, and you'd starch it real stiff and put it inside that brim, is what held it up off of your face. Made it stiffer and better. I guess Eileen does that now, with that extra.

RJM: She said she didn't because sometimes they would sit for a while before they sold and they'd get a line.

LJR: Oh!

RJM: So she didn't usually starch it. Because they would get sort of a line on them after a while.

LJR: Well, I didn't know that.

RJM: She said she used to do it that way. Said she did her own that way.

LJR: Not the ones she sold.

RJM: Right.

LJR: I know we used to starch a piece of some kind of material and sew inside that brim.

RJM: Have you ever seen anyone put a piece of cotton in there, or anything like that? Inside the brim?

LJR: No.

RJM: Just the fabric.

LJR: Just starch it real stiff and that would help keep the bonnet in shape.

RJM: Did you ever make any bonnets out of feed sacks or flour sacks or anything?

LJR: Yes, yes. We used to get feed sacks and flour in printed cotton bags. In fact, I think I made your mother and Patsy both, when they were little, little dresses out of some of those sacks.

RJM: In the early '50s, then you were still using—they were still making those printed cotton bags.

LJR: Some of them were pretty. Kids wore them to school, a lot of them.

RJM: So what else would you make out of the feed sacks and flour sacks—things like children's clothes and bonnets . . .

LJR: And they were good for cup towels. Just owing to the kind of cotton it was.

RJM: It must have been pretty sturdy fabric.

LJR: Yes, it was. Had to, to hold that feed and flour.

RJM: Did you have to do anything else to it—just wash it, or did you have to do anything else to it before you could make something out of it?

LJR: Just wash it and press it, so it'd be smoother to cut your pattern by.

RJM: So once you were older, you probably made some of your own bonnets. Did you ever—how did you get your patterns? Do you remember at all getting a pattern from anywhere?

LJR: From friends. I don't ever remember buying one. I'd just get patterns from different friends of mine.

RJM: So would you just see somebody that had a bonnet you liked and just say, 'Oh, I'd love a pattern'? Is that what would usually happen, or would they tell you, 'I've got a new pattern'? What would you do?

LJR: Well, I'd see their bonnet and like it and ask them for the pattern. I made your mother and Patsy some little bonnets, because I have a picture somewhere of Dana with a little bonnet on. Somewhere in this yard, I remember her with a little bonnet on.

RJM: So you kept wearing bonnets to work in, though, all the way through.

LJR: Mm-hmm.

RJM: You still like to work in a bonnet.

LJR: Yes, work in the garden or my yard, I'd put my bonnet on, instead of a hat.

RJM: So what did you think about bonnets when you were growing up? Did you have any opinion about them?

LJR: Well, I thought some of them were real pretty. And looked dressy-like, but I never did have any real dressy ones, to wear to church; it was just to work in.

RJM: And you still don't want a suntan!

LJR: No.

RJM: That's never been in style with you.

LJR: I'm dark enough already, without getting any darker.

RJM: So did you have any kind of a name for the bonnet with the staves in it, versus the other kind?

LJR: Not really. Just everyday—field, you might say *field*, that would be a good name for them.

RJM: Field bonnets or everyday bonnets.

LJR: Mm-hmm. Work bonnets; they could be named several different things.

RJM: How many bonnets did you usually have when you were little? Just one or did you have more than one at a time?

LJR: I imagine we had more than one; or we could have worn one as long as it lasted and then made another one; I'm not sure what happened, but anyway I know we had those with the staves in them to work in.

RJM: So have you ever decorated any of your bonnets with any trim or anything?

LJR: I think I had some with ruffles around the brim.

RJM: And what would the ruffles be out of?

LJR: The same material.

RJM: Well, I think that's about all my questions. Can you think of anything else—

LJR: That would interest you about them?

RJM: Yes, anything else, or any stories about wearing them, or can you remember any in particular that you ever had?

LJR: I just remember the old stave bonnets that we wore to work in the field in, either chopping cotton or picking cotton or whatever we did in the field.

RJM: That was hard work!

LJR: Yes, it was. We didn't get much pay for it either.

RJM: How much would you get paid for that?

LJR: Well, your granddad and I picked cotton for fifty cents a hundred.

RJM: A hundred pounds.

LJR: A hundred pounds. And I had to work hard to get a hundred pounds in a day. He could pick it—looked so easy for him. He could pick three or four hundred sometimes.

RJM: So who owned the land that you were picking the cotton from?

LJR: Well, different people. My daddy always farmed and his dad did also, so he picked for his dad growing up, then when we got married in April, he had a school in West Texas and it didn't start until later than it did here, so we got out, both of us, and we'd pick cotton all day. Make enough money to carry us out there until he could work a month and make money for teaching. It was rough.

RJM: And when you were younger, everybody picked cotton for your dad's farm?

LJR: Well, just us children. But we picked that year for different people that needed hands to pick cotton to make enough money to go out to his job. He'd been in college, and spent his money going to college. It was rough times back then.

RJM: What year was that, do you know?

LJR: We married in '31.

RJM: So that was right at the early years of the Depression.

LJR: Yes. It was the beginning of the Depression, so jobs were hard to find, and it was rough.

RJM: Did your dad own his land?

LJR: No, he just rented it.

RJM: What was the situation with that? Part of what was made went to the person who owned the land, is that right?

LJR: No, we would pay so much to rent the land, was how that worked.

RJM: So it was just straight rental, not sharecropping?

LJR: Yes; I don't remember how much we had to pay. And the house was just very common. They used to call them shotgun houses. They even had cracks in the walls! Marie was talking, my good friend, she said, land, they lived in houses like that too when she was growing up! She knew all about hard times.

RJM: Was it just boards—just planking?

LJR: Mm-hmm. Some of them were just rough lumber, too. It wasn't just smooth like we have now to deal with, you know. It was—a lot of them was just thrown up with just rough lumber—anything they could get to build a house.

RJM: Not insulated, I take it.

LJR: Oh, goodness, that was insulated with cracks! We'd freeze to death in the winter and burn up in the summer!

RJM: What about the roof? What was that made out of? What was that like?

LJR: Tin, mostly. It wasn't pretty either, just common tin roofing, they called it. They make real pretty ones now. I asked your dad when I had my house roofed last year what he thought about me using the metal roofing, he said no, just the other kind, whatever it's called—

RJM: Just shingles?

LJR: Shingles, was best for my house. But some of the roofing out of metal is pretty, different colors. But it seems like to be it would be awful heavy, to use that metal roofing on a house.

RJM: Probably so. So what did your yard look like then? Did you have a yard area around your house before the fields started?

LJR: Did we do what?

RJM: Did you have a yard?

LJR: Yes, long years ago before we got lawn mowers, we just flat hoed around the house as much as we could. We had dirt yards, no grass.

RJM: Just so it wouldn't be up so tall?

LJR: Didn't have any other way of keeping the weeds and grass down.

RJM: Did you plant anything around the house, then?

LJR: Yes, I know one time when we lived at Pisgah, well, it was a few years after we moved down there, we would flat hoe our whole yard and had the whole thing nearly solid in flowers.

RJM: That sounds pretty.

LJR: It was! But it was work. Oh, to flat hoe that to keep those grass and weeds down! It was something else. But I remember we had so many flowers growing, they made the place look so much better. Is this still recording?

RJM: It was; but I'm going to turn it off now.

Minnie Lee Jumper Skelton

Minnie Lee Skelton (Plate 21) was born on June 3, 1911, in Dobbin, Montgomery County, in northeast Texas. She spent her childhood in the Angelina County community of Hudson, where her family had moved after buying land for farming. Minnie Lee attended the Travathan school and then the Satterwhite Business School. She married Hico Skelton. This interview was conducted on April 7, 2004, at her home in Hudson (outside Lufkin, Texas), where she was still living independently at the age of ninety-two. Minnie Lee died on October 8, 2007.

MLS: Minnie Lee Skelton, narrator

RJM: Rebecca Jumper Matheson, interviewer

[Minnie Lee had displayed two of her sunbonnets for the interviewer to photograph: an older floral one of the slat style, and a blue one with a quilted brim that buttoned to the crown, which she said was from the 1980s.]

RJM: OK—so did you wear sunbonnets when you were growing up?

MLS: Yes. I worked on the farm and had to wear bonnets. We didn't have hats for the ladies back then.

RJM: And you just wore bonnets instead. Did you wear a bonnet when you went to church then?

MLS: No.

RJM: No. Now I see there's a couple of different kinds over here. Do you have names for the—the different kinds? The one with the cardboard in it—do you have any kind of name for that kind of bonnet?

MLS: No, I don't. You'd put it on your head and go to work.

RJM: Now, let's talk about the one with the cardboard in it. Right. What kind of cardboard would you use to put inside there?

MLS: Anything that I could find. Paper wasn't plentiful back in those days. Whatever kind of stiff paper.

RJM: And then when you washed it, what did you do?

MLS: Starched it and ironed it.

RJM: Did you take the cardboard out, or—

MLS: Yes, you'd take the cardboard out to wash it.

RJM: And then you still starched it afterwards, even though you were going to put the cardboard?

MLS: [Yes].

RJM: And the other kind—the other kind does not have those it in.

MLS: Yes. That's the kind of bonnet that you wore to visit.

RJM: Oh, OK. So the other kind, with the cardboard, when did you wear that?

MLS: At the home, in the field, working.

RJM: And the other kind, it would be for visiting?

MLS: Visiting.

RJM: And I see that one has some lace on it, too, so that's a fancier one.

MLS: Right. You wanted it to look nice.

RJM: So what kind of things did you make the bonnet out of? What kind of materials did you usually use?

MLS: Whatever scraps of material you usually had around the house. Usually gingham or—I can't think of the name of the other. It had to be something you could wash, you know.

RJM: Did you use new materials or just . . . ?

MLS: Yes, new materials. Whatever from the scraps that were left over that was enough to use.

RJM: So did you go to town and pick out your fabric, or make it out of whatever was left?

MLS: Whatever was left from the dresses. We made the dresses.

RJM: Now, have you ever sewn a bonnet?

MLS: Yes.

RJM: So you did sew some yourself?

MLS: Yes.

RJM: Who taught you to make bonnets?

MLS: Well, I started sewing when I was a little young girl; by the time I was eighteen I was making my clothes. My mother never learned to sew.

RJM: So did you sew for the whole family then?

MLS: Yes—we had eight children in the family.

RJM: So how many of those were girls? How many did you have to make bonnets for?

MLS: Five were girls, three boys.

RJM: How many bonnets did you usually have at one time?

MLS: Oh, just a bonnet for each one.

RJM: What happened when it wore out, what did you do with it?

MLS: Throw it away. But now that [gestures toward bonnets on dining table] is some that the material has lasted. I can't tell you how old that one is that has the pasteboard. But the other one, oh let me see, that one is from—the eighties.

RJM: So do you have names for the different parts of the bonnet?

MLS: No.

RJM: Did you have a pattern that you used when you sewed your bonnets?

MLS: Yes. It was usually one that the neighbors would let you borrow, and you'd make a bonnet from it.

RJM: So had somebody drawn it up, or were they a bought pattern?

MLS: Well, the ladies back in those days could just sit down and cut out a pattern. Anything! We had an aunt in the family that sewed good, and also Aunt Willie [RJM's great-grandmother].

RJM: So they may have made some patterns?

MLS: Oh, they could just see it in their mind and draw it. Aunt Helen would take a piece of paper and would sit down on the floor and cut a dress pattern, or also a bonnet pattern or whatever.

RJM: So people would just share—if they found a pattern they like, they'd share.

MLS: Uh-huh. We didn't know what it was to buy a pattern in those days.

RJM: OK. So did anyone do anything different to their bonnets or was everyone's pretty much the same?

MLS: Pretty much the same.

RJM: So what was the difference between a dressier bonnet and one for the field, then?

MLS: We called it an everyday bonnet.

RJM: Everyday bonnet. And that was the one you wore out to work in, everyday?

MLS: Yes.

RJM: And what would you call one for dressing up—did you have any name for that?

MLS: No, we didn't.

RJM: So did you make your bonnets on the sewing machine?

MLS: Yes.

RJM: What kind of sewing machine did you have?

MLS: Singer.

RJM: Was it electric or treadle?

MLS: Treadle. We didn't have electric back in those days.

RJM: So what was the main reason for wearing your bonnet?

MLS: Just to protect your face from the hot sun.

RJM: Do you like wearing a bonnet?

MLS: Yes. We perspired a lot.

RJM: So did that help you if you wore your bonnet?

MLS: Stay a little bit cooler.

RJM: Do you remember anybody telling you anything about wearing your bonnet?

MLS: No. We all wore them. And there weren't too many people out here in those days. Up there near where Uncle Charlie and Aunt Willie lived; we lived up on that hill where they were. Uncle Charlie and my daddy came over here from Dobbin, Texas. And Uncle Charlie went to Jacksonville looking for a place and Daddy stopped here in Lufkin and he found this place where Uncle Charlie and him bought. And it was the Carlysle brothers that owned it. Now let me see—I believe they paid $700 for that hundred acres of land. That was in 1913, in January.

RJM: And were you born here?

MLS: No, I was born in Dobbin, Texas.

RJM: What year were you born in?

MLS: 1911. That's Montgomery County, too.

RJM: So most of your growing up you were here.

MLS: Yes. I was born in '11 and we moved in '13 in January, so wasn't but a year old. Can I tell you some of the things about coming over here?

RJM: Yes!

MLS: Uncle Charlie and my daddy—we had to cross two rivers, and one of them didn't have a ferry. We had to cross on and the mules almost drowned pulling the wagon across the river—the first one. And the second one, they had the ferry. You had to pay fifty cents for your wagon, and most of the women stayed in the wagon and crossed. But the men walked, and had to pay a nickel to walk across on the ferry. And a cow cost a nickel to come across, and a hog did, too.

RJM: So what else did you wear when you went out into the field to work? You had your bonnet on—what else did you wear?

MLS: Well, back in those days, I had some overalls that they bought for me. And I worked just like my daddy did. I didn't ever mind working.

RJM: Now, what were you raising back then—what were you—

MLS: Growing? Corn, cotton mostly. Corn, sugar cane, sweet potatoes, peanuts. And we also grew a garden, raised watermelons, cantaloupes.

RJM: Did you wear shoes when you were working outside?

MLS: Yes, but my daddy would go to town to do the shopping, and he would buy my shoes.

RJM: How often did you wash your bonnet?

MLS: Just when they got soiled. Maybe a week or two weeks. We would hang them up when we'd come in the house from working.

RJM: Where did you hang them?

MLS: On a nail on the wall.

RJM: Was that inside the house or outside?

MLS: Uh-huh, inside.

RJM: Did everybody have their own nail, their own bonnet on the wall?

MLS: Some had theirs in the bedroom, some were in the hallway.

RJM: So where was your nail when you came in? Where did you hang yours?

MLS: It was in—we called it the heater room.

RJM: The heater room? What was that?

MLS: Where you had a wood heater, that you put wood in, that would heat and keep everybody warm. The kitchen, of course, had a cook stove. Daddy bought us a "Home Comfort" cook stove, and it had a reservoir on the side, it was on the left hand side. And you'd fill it with water, then you'd have plenty of water that was warm, to bathe in or to add to the vegetables cooking on the stove.

RJM: That must have been easier.

MLS: Yes. We also had a coffee mill. You'd roast it; you know what coffee looks like before it's refined. We would roast that coffee in the oven, then take it out and let it cool, put it in that little coffee grinder, and stand there with our hands and grind the coffee. That's the way we had the coffee.

RJM: Oh, wow. So that must have been hard work!

MLS: No, it wasn't. It was fun to stand and grind there. I don't know who got that coffee grinder. You know things like that you didn't value back in those days, because everybody used them.

RJM: Right. Same thing with sunbonnets—everybody had one.

MLS: Every family—because they made a living off of raising cotton. That was where their money come from.

RJM: Did you ever put any of the cotton you grew into the brims of the bonnets? I've seen some where they put the cotton in there.

MLS: No, we never had a—the bat—to . . .

RJM: To card it?

MLS: The rolls of cotton. There was a Mr. and Mrs. Cane that lived—Lansing at one time owned that land—built a new home there—Mrs. Cane had a—what do you call it? The thing that you put the cotton on and make things?

RJM: OK—spinning wheel?

MLS: Spinning wheel. I'm so sorry.

RJM: No, no! This is great. But you didn't use one?

MLS: We didn't own one.

RJM: Did you ever use any fabric that came from flour sacks?

MLS: Yes. We were very, very thankful to get it, those flour sacks. You bought flour back in those days in twenty-five-pound bags. You also got salt in bags. And let's see, sugar, of course, come in bags. You got five pounds of sugar for about twenty-nine cents, back in those days.

RJM: That's a good deal!

MLS: We didn't have much money back then.

RJM: And what would you use that fabric for? What kinds of things would you make out of a bag like that?

MLS: Oh, [laughter] we made blouses, shirts, underwear—even men's shorts! [laughter]

RJM: So did you—did a lot of those have prints at that time, or were they plain?

MLS: I've got some of the sacks if you want to see them.

RJM: Oh, I'd love to see them.

Afterword
Sunbonnet Collection Care

If you have the privilege to care for sunbonnets in a collection, congratulations! Whether you are the collections manager of a large collection, curator at a small historical society or house museum, or simply the lucky person who found great-grandmother's sunbonnet in an old trunk in the attic, there are special conservation issues to be aware of in caring for this important piece of American history.

Some museum collections have the storage space, manpower, and resources to build individual mounts for each item of millinery in their collections. Mounts sculpted of Ethafoam and covered in stockinet (perhaps even with each sunbonnet in its own individual Coroplast box with a photo on the outside) are a wonderful gift to the objects and affirm a belief in treating every object in our care as an irreplaceable part of our material culture. This may be an ideal storage solution, but it is not available to most collections, where both budgets and storage space are tight.

The sad truth is that in most collections, sunbonnets are a somewhat neglected cousin of the fashionable nineteenth-century bonnet. While a lovely fashionable Leghorn poke bonnet from 1820 may be deemed to merit an individual mount and prime real estate on the storage cabinet shelf, most everyday sunbonnets that have found their way into museum collections sit quietly in out-of-the-way drawers or acid-free storage boxes. As most sunbonnets easily fold flat, they are often piled in drawers, under baby bonnets and caps, to lie in obscurity. This may be because as items of working dress they fall slightly outside the mission and research interests of museums devoted to high fashion. In other cases, twentieth-century sunbonnets are undervalued as "less authentic" than nineteenth-century examples: the loud cotton/polyester fabric of a 1970s daisy print sunbonnet may not fit within preconceived notions of what constitutes a "real" sunbonnet. However, if the object were actually worn and used by a woman working outdoors, its provenance distinguishes it from sunbonnets merely made for pageant or fancy dress purposes, and I would certainly argue that it tells an important story that should be preserved. You may not have the space, money, or time to build mounts for each sunbonnet in your collection, but there are steps you can take to improve their chances of surviving into the next century and beyond.

Even if your sunbonnets must live in a drawer with a number of their fellows, you can take measures to make them "happier." Keep the temperature of your storage space at a year-round 70° F (plus or minus 5° F), and the relative humidity level at 45°–55° F.[1] Make sure that your storage space and drawers are clean and dust-free (dust can cause a variety of problems such as abrasion, retention of moisture and gaseous pollutants on objects, and attraction of insects).[2] Choose the correct kind of archival-quality tissue paper for your sunbonnets, and interleaf this paper between each object.

The vast majority of sunbonnets you will encounter are made of cellulosic materials (plant fibers): occasionally linen, but almost overwhelmingly cotton. Archival tissue papers are available in two varieties, buffered and unbuffered. Choose buffered tissue papers for your cellulosic fiber sunbonnets (unbuffered is better for animal fiber textiles, such as wool or silk). As your cotton sunbonnet ages, it becomes increasingly acidic (pH below neutral 7). Buffered tissue paper has a slightly alkaline pH (above 7) to counteract the acids in aging plant-derived textiles.[3] Buffered tissue paper is available through archival suppliers.

203

Special concerns also arise for slat versus poke-style sunbonnets. Slat sunbonnets often enter collections with the original slats still in place. It is never a good idea to store textile items in contact with wood or cardboard, such as were usually used for slat construction. The wood or cardboard slats are likely to offgas—release harmful acids or other chemicals.[4] Wood or cardboard slats will usually be even more acidic than the cotton surrounding them, and if left in place they will cause further deterioration of the sunbonnet. It would probably be best to very carefully remove the slats and store them separately from the sunbonnet, in a labeled box or container so that the objects remain associated.[5] (The slats should not be thrown away, however. The slats form part of the original object, and the materials used for slats are interesting in and of themselves. Cardboard slats are often recycled from cereal boxes, and so forth, and bear helpful printed information with hints as to their origins.) For exhibition purposes, measure the slat pockets, then cut new slats from acid-free blue board to fill the channels.

For poke-style sunbonnets, many of the care issues arise from the starch used to give stiffness to the sunbonnet brims. One issue is that many insects, such as silverfish, would love to dine on the starch, especially if old-fashioned flour starch was used. Preventive conservation methods, such as frequently cleaning and observing the storage space, monitoring sticky traps, and keeping food and plants out of the area are the best ways to keep insects out of your collection.[6]

As narrator Eileen Johnson observed, starched brims are also very likely to crease when stored flat for a period of time. If your storage space dictates that your sunbonnets must be stored flat, it is very important to pad the fold in the brim with buffered tissue to prevent a permanent crease from forming. A small tissue "cigar" will serve this purpose: take a sheet of tissue paper and gather it in your hands a bit at a time until you have formed a somewhat free-form accordion shape. Place this tissue against the area where the brim would fold, so that now you have a gentle curve rather than an abrupt fold.

For both types of sunbonnet, other areas also require special attention. If the crown is full, for example, this section of the sunbonnet should be lightly padded out with tissue. Properly padding your sunbonnets will mean that fewer of them will fit in a box or drawer, but it is well worth the inconvenience. Also, remember that tissue paper and archival storage boxes do not remain acid-free forever; these materials should be replaced every few years.

Ties and the interior sections of the sunbonnet that were in contact with the face often have perspiration stains. Since most everyday sunbonnets were well-worn, they are often brought into collections extremely dirty. Assuming that any dyes in the fabric are stable, a gentle wet cleaning (cold water and a tiny amount of

Orvus paste) may be useful to remove stains and acidic particulates that could lead to textile damage.[7]

As a fashion historian, one of the most frequently asked questions I receive is some variation on the following: "What is the best way for me to display my great-grandmother's christening gown/baby dress/wedding gown?" This is the first sentence. It is almost immediately followed by a second sentence, which invariably begins with, "I thought I would . . ."

"I thought I would put it in a shadow box."

"I thought I would hang it from this antique pegboard shelf."

"I thought I would display it on my dressmaker's dummy."

The truth is, they have already made up their minds what they are going to do, and they just want an official stamp of approval for the plan. When I explain that exposure to ordinary light (sunlight or even the lights in your home) is one of the most damaging things you could do to a textile object,[8] and that if you would truly like to preserve this piece you must not put it on permanent display, the response is almost always one of disappointment, yet determination to go on with their display plans.

Of course, as long as you own an object privately, the decision as to how to treat the object is up to you. You may wear your mother's rare Dior couture evening gown to the local charity ball, you may let your children play dress-up in your great-grandmother's Lucile teagown, you may put your elbow through the Picasso in your office (as Steve Wynn famously did), and you may throw your grandmother's sunbonnet in the washing machine, then wear it while pruning your rose bushes. However, you cannot expect an art historian or conservator to approve. As textile conservator Harold F. Mailand concludes, "[T]he two goals of preservation and use are diametrically opposed."[9]

If you are ready to participate in the next chapter of sunbonnet history, my suggestion would be to keep the vintage sunbonnets in your collection safely in storage and either sew a new sunbonnet for yourself or have one made. In addition to the patterns available in the Appendix of this book, Denise Dreher offers patterns of nineteenth-century bonnet styles in *From the Neck Up: An Illustrated Guide to Hatmaking*.[10] (Note: Dreher's patterns do not include ties.)

Appendix

The following patterns are included primarily as a tool to help the reader understand basic sunbonnet construction. The patterns were taken from extant twentieth-century sunbonnets. Readers wishing to use these patterns to sew their own sunbonnets should be cautioned that these are only a general guide, and do not include seam allowances. In addition, everyday sunbonnets worn and used by working farm women are full of internal variations: the ties are longer on one side than the other, the seam allowances are uneven, two different scraps may have been sewn together to make a single pattern piece; in short, because of the utilitarian/make-do-and-reuse nature of sunbonnets, they often demonstrate a freewheeling approach to construction. The reader should feel free to do the same, remembering that the pieces might need to be adjusted for head size and personal preference.

A Very Simple Slat Sunbonnet from the 1940s

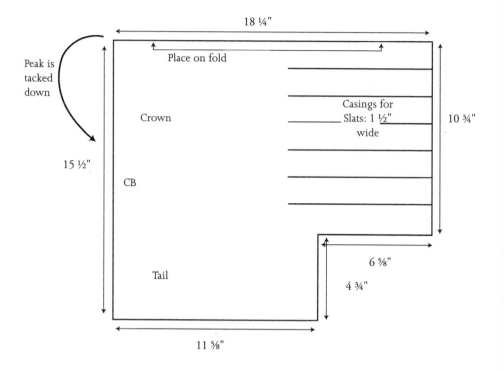

18 ¼"

Place on fold

Peak is tacked down

Crown

Casings for Slats: 1 ½" wide

10 ¾"

15 ½"

CB

Tail

6 ⅝"

4 ¾"

11 ⅝"

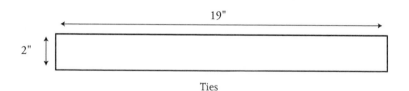

19"

2"

Ties

The sunbonnet is dated based on its slats—pieces of
cardboard cut from a Post Toasties cereal box that refers
to sugar rationing and suggests sweetening the cereal
with the syrup from canned peaches instead.

Scale ³⁄₁₆" = 1"
Cut one of bonnet on fold of fabric.
Cut four ties.

Pattern by Rebecca Matheson
Technical Illustration by Kristen Stewart

Star Caldwell's Grandmother's Convertible Apron/Sunbonnet

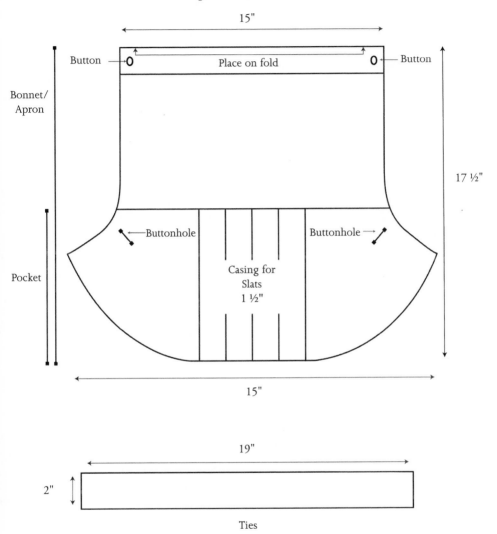

Ties

This pattern creats a sunbonnet similar to Louise Rusk's clothespin apron/bonnet (Figure numbers 18 and 19)

Scale: ³⁄₁₆" = 1"
Cut one of entire bonnet/apron on fold of fabric.
Cut one of pocket.
Cut two ties.

Pattern by Star Caldwell
Technical Illustration by Kristen Stewart

A Poke-Style Visiting Sunbonnet
(For photograph see Plate 11)

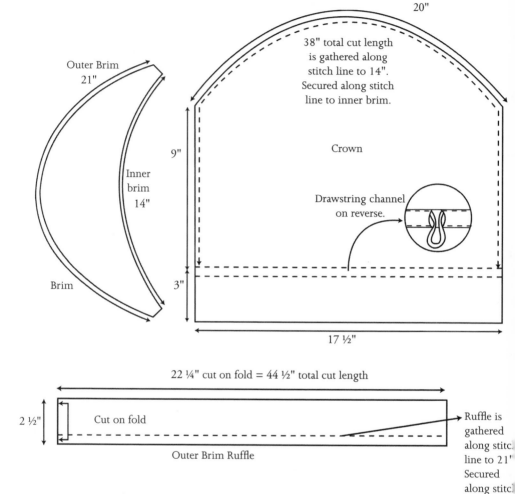

20"

Outer Brim
21"

38" total cut length
is gathered along
stitch line to 14".
Secured along stitch
line to inner brim.

Inner
brim
14"

9"

Crown

Drawstring channel
on reverse.

Brim

3"

17 ½"

22 ¼" cut on fold = 44 ½" total cut length

2 ½"

Cut on fold

Outer Brim Ruffle

Ruffle is
gathered
along stitc[h]
line to 21"
Secured
along stitc[h]
line to out[er]
brim

2 ¼"

Folded and stitched

Ties

Scale: ³⁄₁₆" = 1"
Cut one of each: crown, outer brim ruffle
Cut two of each: brim, ties
Cut one in interlining: brim

Pattern by Kristen Stewart
Technical Illustration by Kristen Stewart

Notes

Introduction

1. Neal Gabler, *Walt Disney: The Triumph of American Imagination* (New York: Alfred A. Knopf, 2006), 514–515.

2. R. Turner Wilcox, *The Mode in Hats and Headdress* (New York: Charles Scribner's Sons, 1945), 215.

3. Betty J. Mills, *Calico Chronicle* (Lubbock: Texas Tech University Press, 1985), 52–57; Janet K. Jeffery, "The Sunbonnet as Folk Costume," in *Corners of Texas*, Francis Edward Abernethy, ed. Publication of the Texas Folklore Society LII (Denton: University of North Texas Press, 1993), 208–219; Fiona Clark, *Hats* (London: Batsford, 1982), 27.

4. Aileen Ribeiro, *Fashion and Fiction: Dress in Art and Literature in Stuart England* (New Haven, CT: Yale University Press, 2005), 1.

5. Thomas J. Schlereth, "Material Culture and Cultural Research," in *Material Culture: A Research Guide*, ed. Thomas J. Schlereth (Lawrence: University Press of Kansas, 1985), 3.

6. Jules David Prown, "The Truth of Material Culture: History or Fiction?" in *History from Things: Essays on Material Culture*, ed. Steven Lubar and W. David Kingery (Washington, DC: Smithsonian Institution Press, 1995), 1–19.

7. Donald A. Ritchie, *Doing Oral History* (New York: Twayne, 1995), 207–209.

8. George Ewart Evans, "Dress and the Rural Historian," *Costume* 8 (1974), 39.

9. Ibid., 39.

10. Ibid., 40.

11. Thad Sitton, ed., *The Loblolly Book* (Austin: Texas Monthly Press, 1983), 73–75. For an example of a nonscholarly work that takes its material from these interviews, see Tumbleweed Smith, *Under the Chinaberry Tree* (Austin: Eakin Press, 2002), 79–80.

12. Narrator Eileen Johnson's name was changed to protect her privacy, here and throughout.

13. Hilda Amphlett, *Hats: A History of Fashion in Headwear* (Mineola, NY: Dover, 2003), 164; Diana De Marly, *Working Dress: A History of Occupational Clothing* (New York: Holmes & Meier, 1986), 109, 140–141; Woman's Institute of Domestic Arts and Sciences, Ltd., *Fancy Aprons and Sunbonnets* (London: International Educational Publishing Company, 1916), 41–60.

14. Lucy Maud Montgomery, *Anne of the Island* (Philadelphia: Running Press, 1997), 41.

15. Louise Jenkins Rusk, interview by author, April 9, 2004, Lufkin, Texas.

16. Jeffery, "The Sunbonnet as Folk Costume," 214.

17. Mrs. Ruby Youngblood, "Sunbonnets," in *The Loblolly Book: Water Witching, Wild Hog Hunting, Home Remedies, Grandma's Moral Tales and Other Affairs of Plain Texas Living*, ed. Thad Sitton (Austin: Texas Monthly Press, 1983),

75; Louise Jenkins Rusk interview, April 9, 2004; Faye Rusk, interview by author, April 6, 2004, Nacogdoches, Texas.

18. Louise Jenkins Rusk interview, April 9, 2004.

19. Ibid.; R. Youngblood, "Sunbonnets," 75.

20. Jeffery, "The Sunbonnet as Folk Costume," 212; Betty J. Mills, *Calico Chronicle*, 54, 57.

21. Faye Rusk interview, April 6, 2004; Louise Jenkins Rusk interview, April 9, 2004; R. Youngblood, "Sunbonnets," 75.

Chapter 1

1. Phyllis G. Tortora, ed., *Fairchild's Dictionary of Textiles*, 7th ed. (New York: Fairchild, 2000), 211.

2. Lourdes M. Font and Trudie A. Grace, *The Gilded Age: High Fashion and Society in the Hudson Highlands, 1865–1914* (Cold Spring, NY: Putnam County Historical Society & Foundry School Museum, 2006), 26.

3. Jeffery, "The Sunbonnet as Folk Costume," 211.

4. Georgine de Courtais, *Women's Headdresses and Hairstyles in England from AD 600 to the Present Day* (London: Batsford, 1986), 92; C. Willett Cunnington, Phillis Cunnington, and Charles Beard, *A Dictionary of English Costume* (London: Adam and Charles Black, 1960), 34; Katherine M. Lester and Rose N. Kerr, *Historic Costume* (Peoria, IL: Bennett, 1977), 179, 181.

5. Lester and Kerr, *Historic Costume*, 179.

6. Elizabeth Gaskell, *Cranford* (London: Penguin Books, 1986), 110.

7. Linda Grant de Pauw and Conover Hunt, *"Remember the Ladies":Women in America, 1750–1815* (New York: Viking, 1976), 113.

8. De Marly, *Working Dress*, 141.

9. David Hackett Fischer, *Albion's Seed: Four British Folkways in America* (New York and Oxford: Oxford University Press, 1989), 734.

10. Linda Baumgarten, *Eighteenth-Century Clothing at Williamsburg* (Williamsburg, VA: The Colonial Williamsburg Foundation, 2002), 40.

11. Gerilyn Tandberg, "Confederate Bonnets: Imagination and Ingenuity," *Dress* 32 (2005): 18.

12. de Courtais, *Women's Headdresses and Hairstyles*, 82.

13. Amphlett, *Hats*, 199.

14. Philippe Perrot, *Fashioning the Bourgeoisie: A History of Clothing in the Nineteenth Century*, trans. Richard Bienvenu (Princeton, NJ: Princeton University Press, 1994), 104; Joan Severa, *Dressed for the Photographer: Ordinary Americans and Fashion, 1840–1900* (Kent, OH, and London: Kent State University Press, 1995), 10.

15. Wilcox, *The Mode in Hats and Headdress*, 215.

16. de Courtais, *Women's Headdresses and Hairstyles*, 118.

17. Cunnington, Cunnington, and Beard, *A Dictionary of English Costume*, 223; de Courtais, *Women's Headdresses and Hairstyles*, 108

18. de Courtais, *Women's Headdresses and Hairstyles*, 100.

19. Althea Mackenzie, *Buttons and Trimmings* (London: The National Trust, 2004), 44.

20. Anne Bissonette, *Early Neoclassical Hairstyles: 1750–1790*, paper presented as part of the symposium "The Many Layered Meanings of Costume" at the annual meeting of the Costume Society of America Southeast Region, Williamsburg, VA, October 31–November 2, 2008.

21. Clark, *Hats*, 28.

22. de Courtais, *Women's Headdresses and Hairstyles*, 95.

23. Clark, *Hats*, 25; de Courtais, *Women's Headdresses and Hairstyles*, 108.

24. Mackenzie, *Buttons and Trimmings*, 56.

25. Richard Martin, *Our New Clothes: Acquisitions of the 1990s* (New York: The Metropolitan Museum of Art, 1999), 26.

26. Clark, *Hats*, 25; de Courtais, *Women's Headdresses and Hairstyles*, 108.

27. Clark, *Hats,* 27.

28. Mackenzie, *Buttons and Trimmings,* 62.

29. Clark, *Hats,* 29.

30. Tandberg, "Confederate Bonnets," 18.

31. Clark, *Hats,* 29.

32. Ibid., 86.

33. Mrs. Odell Youngblood, "Sunbonnets," in *The Loblolly Book: Water Witching, Wild Hog Hunting, Home Remedies, Grandma's Moral Tales and Other Affairs of Plain Texas Living,* ed. Thad Sitton (Austin: Texas Monthly Press, 1983), 74.

Chapter 2

1. Lawrence M. Friedman, *The History of American Law* (New York: Touchstone, 1985), 232.

2. Sally I. Helvenston, "Fashion and Function in Women's Dress in Rural New England, 1840–1900," *Dress* 18 (1991), 28.

3. Quoted in Helvenston, "Fashion and Function in Women's Dress," 27.

4. Arthur Meier Schlesinger, *The Rise of the City, 1878–1898* (Columbus: Ohio State University Press, 1999), 61.

5. Prown, "The Truth of Material Culture," 1.

6. Ibid., 13.

7. Helvenston, "Fashion and Function in Women's Dress," 28.

8. Andrew Bolton, *Men in Skirts* (London: V&A Publications, 2003), 61.

9. Fischer, *Albion's Seed,* 606.

10. Ibid., 735.

11. Ibid., 759.

12. Dilue Rose Harris, "Dilue Rose Harris," in *Texas Tears and Texas Sunshine,* ed. Jo Ellen Exley (College Station: Texas A&M University Press, 1985), 61.

13. Ibid., 62.

14. Ibid., 65.

15. Mark Twain, *Adventures of Huckleberry Finn* (New York: Harper & Row, 1987), 78.

16. Mills, *Calico Chronicle*, 7, 52.

17. Twain, *Huckleberry Finn*, 83.

18. Ibid., 83–84, 89.

19. Ibid., 84.

20. Ibid., 85.

21. Clark, *Hats*, 86.

22. Carrie A. Hall and Rose G. Kretsinger, *The Romance of the Patchwork Quilt in America* (New York: Bonanza, 1935), 258.

23. Mills, *Calico Chronicle*, 53.

24. Twain, *Huckleberry Finn*, 83.

25. Pat Earnshaw, *A Dictionary of Lace* (Mineola, NY: Dover, 1999), 223.

26. Twain, *Huckleberry Finn*, 91.

27. Mills, *Calico Chronicle*, 56.

28. Bell Irwin Wiley, *Confederate Women: Beyond the Petticoat* (New York: Barnes and Noble, 1994), 46.

29. Ibid., 47.

30. Elliott West, *Growing Up with the Country: Childhood on the Far Western Frontier* (Albuquerque: University of New Mexico Press, 1989), 246.

31. Ibid.

32. Ibid., 247–249.

33. Willa Cather, *O Pioneers!* (New York: Barnes and Noble Classics, 2003), 88.

34. Ibid., 27.

35. Ibid., 47.

36. "The Vogue of the Sunbonnet," *New York Times*, June 21, 1903.

37. Helvenston, "Fashion and Function in Women's Dress," 32, quoting Frances H. Perry, "Enlarged Shade Hats for Out-Door Workers," *American Agriculturalist* 48 (August 1889): 398.

38. Wilcox, *The Mode in Hats and Headdress*, 213.

39. Helvenston, "Fashion and Function in Women's Dress," 32, quoting Annie G. Hale, "Ch. XI. Women's Work Among the Garden Plants," *New England Farmer* 2 (June 1868): 294.

40. Joan M. Jensen, *With These Hands: Women Working on the Land* (Old Westbury, NY: The Feminist Press/McGraw-Hill, 1981), 34.

41. Wilcox, *The Mode in Hats and Headdress*, 213.

42. Tandberg, "Confederate Bonnets," 21.

43. Woman's Institute of Domestic Arts and Sciences, Ltd., *Fancy Aprons and Sunbonnets*, 42.

44. This was calculated using the unskilled wage index. Samuel H. Williamson, "An Index of the Wage of Unskilled Labor from 1774 to the Present" Economic History Services, December 2004, www.eh.net/hmit/databases/unskilledwage (accessed November 11, 2008).

45. E. Butterick & Co.'s *Summer Catalogue 1882* (New York: Butterick, 1882), in *American Dress Pattern Catalogues, 1873–1909*, ed. Nancy Villa Bryk (New York: Dover, 1988), 58.

Chapter 3

1. Jeffery, "The Sunbonnet as Folk Costume," 216.

2. Baumgarten, *What Clothes Reveal*, 31.

3. Ibid.

4. "The Vogue of the Sunbonnet," *New York Times*, June 21, 1903.

5. Ibid.

6. Ibid.

7. Minnie Lee Skelton, interview by author, April 7, 2004, Lufkin, Texas.

8. Louise Jenkins Rusk interview, April 9, 2004.

9. Eileen Johnson, sunbonnet maker and seller, Nacogdoches Trade Days flea market, interview by author, January 4, 2004, Nacogdoches, Texas.

10. *E. Butterick & Co.'s Summer Catalogue 1882*, 58.

11. Louise Jenkins Rusk interview, April 9, 2004; Minnie Lee Skelton interview, April 7, 2004.

12. R. Youngblood, "Sunbonnets," 75.

13. Joanne W. Thompson, home economist, letter to author, dated June 2004.

14. Terri Jones, "Sunbonnets," *Bittersweet IV*, no. 4 (Summer 1977): 26.

15. Julia Brazil, interview by author, April 7, 2004, Lufkin, Texas; Minnie Lee Skelton interview, April 7, 2004.

16. Eileen Johnson interview, January 4, 2004.

17. R. Youngblood, "Sunbonnets," 75.

18. Eileen Johnson interview, January 4, 2004.

19. Jeffery, "The Sunbonnet as Folk Costume," 215.

20. Mills, *Calico Chronicle*, 56.

21. Julia Brazil interview, April 7, 2004; Louise Jenkins Rusk interview, April 9, 2004; Minnie Lee Skelton interview, April 7, 2004.

22. R. Youngblood, "Sunbonnets," 75.

23. Faye Rusk interview, April 6, 2004.

24. Julia Brazil interview, April 7, 2004; Minnie Lee Skelton interview, April 7, 2004.

25. Minnie Lee Skelton interview, April 7, 2004.

26. Faye Rusk interview, April 6, 2004.

27. Julia Brazil interview, April 7, 2004.

28. Jeffery, "The Sunbonnet as Folk Costume," 215; Louise Jenkins Rusk interview, April 9, 2004; Minnie Lee Skelton interview, April 7, 2004; Faye Rusk interview, April 6, 2004.

29. George Ewing, "Forked Stick Folkcraft," in Corners of Texas, ed. Francis Edward Abernethy, publication of the Texas Folklore Society LII (Denton: University of North Texas Press, 1993), 109.

30. Faye Rusk interview, April 6, 2004.

31. Louise Jenkins Rusk interview, April 9, 2004.

32. Faye Rusk interview, April 6, 2004.

Chapter 4

1. Jeffery, "The Sunbonnet as Folk Costume," 213.

2. de Courtais, Women's Headdresses and Hairstyles, 100.

3. Eileen Johnson interview, January 4, 2004.

4. Jeffery, "The Sunbonnet as Folk Costume," 213.

5. Woman's Institute of Domestic Arts and Sciences, Ltd., Fancy Aprons and Sunbonnets, 42.

6. Lelia Evie Dorsett Rusk, 1883–1956, lived in Nacogdoches County, Texas, and is the author's great-grandmother.

7. Ruby Isabelle Turner Duke, 1886–1968, spent much of her life in Northeast Texas, as well as farther south in Angelina County, Texas, and is the author's great-grandmother.

8. Jeffery, "The Sunbonnet as Folk Costume," 212.

9. Ibid., 215; Mills, Calico Chronicle, 54.

10. Julia Brazil interview, April 7, 2004; Louise Jenkins Rusk interview, April 9, 2004.

11. Woman's Institute of Domestic Arts and Sciences, Ltd., *Fancy Aprons and Sunbonnets,* 46.

12. Faye Rusk interview, April 6, 2004.

13. Roderick Kiracofe and Mary Elizabeth Johnson, *The American Quilt: A History of Cloth and Comfort 1750–1950* (New York: Clarkson Potter, 1993), 9.

14. Faye Rusk interview, April 6, 2004; Minnie Lee Skelton interview, April 7, 2004.

15. Faye Rusk interview, April 6, 2004.

16. Jeffery, "The Sunbonnet as Folk Costume," 215; Mills, *Calico Chronicle,* 56.

17. Faye Rusk interview, April 6, 2004.

18. Louise Jenkins Rusk interview, April 9, 2004.

19. Faye Rusk interview, April 6, 2004.

20. Pearl Lowe Boyd, "From My Kitchen Window" column, *The Dunedin Times,* Dunedin, FL, 1950, in *Sunbonnets and Sweet Gum,* ed. Pearl Lowe Boyd and John Allen Boyd (Philadelphia: by the author via Xlibris, 2001), 11; Woman's Institute of Domestic Arts and Sciences, Ltd., *Fancy Aprons and Sunbonnets,* 53.

21. Louise Jenkins Rusk interview, April 9, 2004.

22. Woman's Institute of Domestic Arts and Sciences, Ltd., *Fancy Aprons and Sunbonnets,* 48.

23. Jones, "Sunbonnets," 26.

24. Ibid.

25. Ibid.

26. Woman's Institute of Domestic Arts and Sciences, Ltd., *Fancy Aprons and Sunbonnets,* 47.

27. Louise Jenkins Rusk interview, January 1, 2004.

28. R. Youngblood, "Sunbonnets," 75.

29. Louise Jenkins Rusk interview, April 9, 2004; Faye Rusk interview, April 6, 2004.

30. Merritt Ierley, *The Comforts of Home: The American House and the Evolution of Modern Convenience* (New York: Three Rivers, 1999), 236.

31. Illinois State Museum, *At Home in a House Divided: 1850–1880*, December 31, 1996, www.museum.state.il.us/exhibits/athome/1850/objects/sadiron.htm (accessed October 13, 2007).

32. Ierley, *The Comforts of Home*, 236.

33. Faye Rusk interview, April 6, 2004.

34. R. Youngblood, "Sunbonnets," 75.

35. Faye Rusk interview, April 6, 2004.

36. Ibid.

37. Jeffery, "The Sunbonnet as Folk Costume," 212; O. Youngblood, "Sunbonnets," 74.

38. Minnie Lee Skelton interview, April 7, 2004.

39. Louise Jenkins Rusk interview, April 9, 2004.

40. O. Youngblood, "Sunbonnets," 74.

41. Jeffery, "The Sunbonnet as Folk Costume," 215.

42. Minnie Lee Skelton interview, April 7, 2004.

43. Louise Jenkins Rusk interview, April 9, 2004.

44. Faye Rusk interview, April 6, 2004.

45. Woman's Institute of Domestic Arts and Sciences, Ltd., *Fancy Aprons and Sunbonnets*, 43.

46. "Roadside Holiday, U.S.A." *Vogue* (March 1, 1954): 152.

47. de Courtais, *Women's Headdresses and Hairstyles*, 84; Ray Emerson Stryker and Nancy Wood, *In This Proud Land: America 1935–1943 as Seen in the FSA Photographs* (New York: Galahad, 1973), 58, 113.

48. Eileen Johnson interview, January 4, 2004.

49. United Pentecostal Church International, "The Scriptures Decree Modesty in Dress," www.upci.org/doctrine/scripturesModesty.asp (accessed October 12, 2007).

50. Louise Jenkins Rusk interview, April 9, 2004.

51. Faye Rusk interview, April 6, 2004.

52. Ibid.

53. Boyd, "From My Kitchen Window," 11.

54. Jeffery, "The Sunbonnet as Folk Costume," 212.

55. Mills, *Calico Chronicle*, 54.

56. Julia Brazil interview, April 7, 2004.

57. Faye Rusk interview, April 6, 2004.

Chapter 5

1. Faye Rusk interview, April 6, 2004; O. Youngblood, "Sunbonnets," 74.

2. Minnie Lee Skelton interview, April 7, 2004.

3. Julia Brazil interview, April 7, 2004.

4. O. Youngblood, "Sunbonnets," 74.

5. Louise Jenkins Rusk interview, April 9, 2004; Minnie Lee Skelton interview, April 7, 2004.

6. Jones, "Sunbonnets," 25.

7. Louise Rusk interview, O. Youngblood, "Sunbonnets," 74.

8. Boyd, "From My Kitchen Window," 10.

9. Eileen Johnson interview, January 4, 2004.

10. Boyd, "From My Kitchen Window," 10.

11. Faye Rusk interview, April 6, 2004.

12. Julia Brazil interview, April 7, 2004.

13. Faye Rusk interview, April 6, 2004.

14. Louise Jenkins Rusk interview, April 9, 2004.

15. Boyd, "From My Kitchen Window," 12.

16. Woman's Institute of Domestic Arts and Sciences, Ltd., *Fancy Aprons and Sunbonnets*, 54.

Chapter 6

1. Faye Rusk interview, April 6, 2004.

2. Minnie Lee Skelton interview, April 7, 2004.

3. Faye Rusk interview, April 6, 2004; Louise Jenkins Rusk interview, April 7, 2004; Minnie Lee Skelton interview, April 7, 2004.

4. Louise Jenkins Rusk interview, April 7, 2004.

5. Minnie Lee Skelton interview, April 7, 2004.

6. Betty Jumper, electronic mail to author, dated October 6, 2003.

7. Susan Strawn, Jane Farrell-Beck, and Ann R. Hemken, "Bib Overalls: Function and Fashion," *Dress* 32 (2005): 43.

8. Ibid., 44, 46.

9. Louise Jenkins Rusk interview, April 7, 2004.

10. Minnie Lee Skelton interview, April 7, 2004.

11. Jensen, *With These Hands*, 205–206, quoting Margaret Hagood, *Mothers of the South: Portraiture of the White Tenant Farm Woman* (1939, reprinted New York: Norton, 1977).

12. Fischer, *Albion's Seed*, 676.

13. Louise Jenkins Rusk interview, April 9, 2004.

14. Minnie Lee Skelton interview, April 7, 2004; Faye Rusk interview, April 6, 2004.

15. Julia Brazil interview, April 7, 2004.

16. Faye Rusk interview, April 6, 2004.

17. Eddie Stimpson, Jr., *My Remembers: A Black Sharecropper's Recollections of the Depression* (Denton: University of North Texas Press, 1996), 46.

18. Erskine Caldwell, *Tobacco Road* (Athens: University of Georgia Press, 1995), 75.

19. Louise Jenkins Rusk interview, April 9, 2004.

20. Minnie Lee Skelton interview, April 7, 2004.

21. Faye Rusk interview, April 6, 2004.

22. Stryker and Wood, *In This Proud Land*, 187.

23. Sheila ffolliott, "Learning to Be Looked At: A Portrait of (the Artist as) a Young Woman in Agnès Merlet's *Artemisia*," in *Reclaiming Female Agency: Feminist Art History After Postmodernism*, ed. Norma Broude and Mary D. Garrard (Berkeley: University of California Press, 2005), 49.

24. Claudia Brush Kidwell, with Nancy Rexford, "Foreword," in *Dressed for the Photographer: Ordinary Americans and Fashion, 1840–1900* by Joan Severa (Kent, OH, and London: Kent State University Press, 1995), xiii.

25. Anne Hollander, *Seeing Through Clothes* (Berkeley: University of California Press, 1993), 349.

26. Lady Duff Gordon, *Discretions and Indiscretions* (London: Jarrolds, 1932), 76.

27. Julia Brazil interview, April 7, 2004.

28. Louise Jenkins Rusk interview, April 9, 2004.

29. J. B. Smallwood, Jr., "Cotton, Cattle, and Crude: The Texas Economy, 1865–1980," in *Texas Country: The Changing Rural Scene*, ed. Glen E. Lich and Dona B. Reeves-Marquardt (College Station: Texas A&M University Press, 1986), 85.

30. This also demonstrates the difficulty of dating sunbonnets. Even as the twentieth century progressed, and textiles became less expensive and valuable, many East Texas women continued to treasure every scrap of material in a scrap basket. Sunbonnets are often made of fabric scraps, which may have been in a woman's scrap basket for years before being

incorporated into a sunbonnet. Therefore, the date of construction is not always readily apparent from the date of the fabric.

31. Jeffery, "The Sunbonnet as Folk Costume," 212.

32. Joyce Cheney, *Aprons: Icons of the American Home* (Philadelphia: Running Press, 2000), 87.

Chapter 7

1. R. Youngblood, "Sunbonnets," 75.

2. Minnie Lee Skelton interview, April 7, 2004.

3. Julia Brazil interview, April 7, 2004.

4. Jones, "Sunbonnets," 25.

5. Woman's Institute of Domestic Arts and Sciences, Ltd., *Fancy Aprons and Sunbonnets*, 41.

6. Minnie Lee Skelton interview, April 7, 2004.

7. Julia Brazil interview, April 7, 2004.

8. Faye Rusk interview, April 6, 2004.

9. Eileen Johnson interview, January 4, 2004.

10. Faye Rusk interview, April 6, 2004.

11. Ibid.

12. Louise Jenkins Rusk interview, April 9, 2004.

13. Julia Brazil interview, April 7, 2004.

14. Jones, "Sunbonnets," 25.

15. Caroline Rennolds Milbank, *New York Fashion: The Evolution of American Style* (New York: Abrams, 1989), 179.

16. Virginia Pope, "Lilly Daché Puts New Theory on Dressing into Her Exhibit," *New York Times*, September 23, 1954, 41.

17. "Hair Cut on 'Bias' Marks Daché Look," *New York Times*, July 15, 1958, 19.

18. Hamish Bowles, *Jacqueline Kennedy: The White House Years* (New York: The Metropolitan Museum of Art and Bulfinch, 2001), 63.

Chapter 8

1. Aileen Ribeiro, *Dress and Morality* (Oxford: Berg, 2003), 73.

2. Ibid., 107, 109.

3. There is an interesting parallel between the nineteenth-century bonnet's function to hide the wearer's face from the sun and the style for fashionable Victorian homes to be thickly hung with curtains, which prevented the sun's rays from making inroads against the interiors. See Judith Flanders, *Inside the Victorian Home: A Portrait of Domestic Life in Victorian England* (New York: Norton, 2004), 192.

4. Meredith Etherington-Smith and Jeremy Pilcher, *The "It" Girls: Elinor Glyn, Novelist, and Her Sister Lucile, Couturière* (New York: Harcourt Brace Jovanovich, 1986), 65.

5. Edmonde Charles-Roux, *Chanel and Her World* (New York: Vendome, 1981), 109.

6. Thorstein Veblen, *The Theory of the Leisure Class* (New York: Dover, 1994), 105.

7. Perrot, *Fashioning the Bourgeoisie*, 102.

8. Laura Ingalls Wilder, *Little House on the Prairie* (New York: Harper Trophy, 1971), 122.

9. Faye Rusk interview, April 6, 2004.

10. Boyd, "From My Kitchen Window," 11.

11. Louise Jenkins Rusk interview, April 9, 2004.

12. Charles-Roux, *Chanel and Her World*, 109.

13. Perrot, *Fashioning the Bourgeoisie*, 103.

14. This same principle seemed to be at work in the early 2000s in regards to hosiery, as women in the freezing temperatures of New York winters went hosiery-free and in sandals—a style boasting of the priv-

ilege of a driver always waiting at the curb—while Southern women sweated through searing summer heat in the modesty of pantyhose.

15. Charles-Roux, *Chanel and Her World*, 109.

16. Louise Jenkins Rusk interview, April 9, 2004.

17. Faye Rusk interview, April 6, 2004.

18. Ana Castillo, "We Would Like You to Know," in *My Father Was a Toltec and Selected Poems* (New York: Norton, 1995), 82, stanza 6.

19. José F. Aranda, Jr., *When We Arrive: A New Literary History of Mexican America* (Tucson: University of Arizona Press, 2003), 10.

20. Ibid., 5.

21. Richard Rodriguez, *Hunger of Memory: The Education of Richard Rodriguez* (New York: Bantam, 1982), 114–115.

22. Ibid., 113.

23. Jeffery, "The Sunbonnet as Folk Costume," 216.

24. Linda Baumgarten, *What Clothes Reveal: The Language of Clothing in Colonial and Federal America* (New Haven, CT: The Colonial Williamsburg Foundation and Yale University Press, 2002), 138.

25. Helen Bradley Foster, "New Raiments of Self": African American Clothing in the Antebellum South (Oxford: Berg, 1997), 255.

26. Ibid., 257.

27. Tandberg, "Confederate Bonnets," 15, quoting George P. Rawick, ed., *Georgia Narratives*, Part 1, vol. 3, *The American Slave: A Composite Biography: Supplement*, Series I (1941; reprint, Westport, CT: Greenwood, 1974), 181–182.

28. Foster, *"New Raiments of Self,"* 257.

29. Library of Congress Prints and Photographs Division, call number Lot 11930, no. 247 [P&P], reproduction number LC-USZ62-103813 (b&w film copy neg.). "Three women and one man hoeing in field," 1899 or 1900.

30. Lalita Tademy, *Cane River* (New York: Warner Books, 2001), 406.

31. Peter Wollen, *Raiding the Icebox: Reflections on Twentieth-Century Culture* (Bloomington and Indianapolis: University of Indiana Press, 1993), 20.

32. Faye Rusk interview, April 6, 2004.

Chapter 9

1. Helvenston, "Fashion and Function in Women's Dress," 27.

2. Arthur Meier Schlesinger, *The Rise of the City, 1878–1898* (Columbus: Ohio State University Press, 1999), 2.

3. Clarence C. Schultz, "Whatever Happened to the Little Frame House on the Prairie?" in *Texas Country: The Changing Rural Scene*, ed. Glen E. Lich and Dona B. Reeves-Marquardt (College Station: Texas A&M University Press, 1986), 112.

4. Jeffery, "The Sunbonnet as Folk Costume," 217.

5. Louise Jenkins Rusk interview, April 9, 2004.

6. Faye Rusk interview, April 6, 2004.

7. Ibid.

8. Ibid.; Louise Jenkins Rusk interview, April 9, 2004.

9. Faye Rusk interview, April 6, 2004.

10. Dorothy Draper, *Entertaining Is Fun!: How to Be a Popular Hostess* (New York: Rizzoli, 2004), 1.

11. Ibid., 96.

12. "Roadside Holiday, U.S.A.," 152.

13. Julia Brazil interview, April 7, 2004.

14. Eileen Johnson interview, January 4, 2004.

15. Ibid.

16. For example, see "How to Sew a Sunbonnet," www.ehow.com/how_2077833_sew-sunbonnet.html (accessed October 16, 2007).

17. Betty Callahan, "Make Your Own Sunbonnet . . . in Less than Two Hours," *Mother Earth News: The Original Guide to Living Wisely*, July/August 1978, http://www.motherearthnews.com/DIY/1978-07-01/Make-Your-Own-Sunbonnet-in-Less-Than-Two-Hours.aspx (accessed October 16, 2007).

18. Penelope J. Corfield, "Dress for Deference and Dissent: Hats and the Decline of Hat Honor," *Costume* 23 (1989): 71.

Afterword

1. Harold F. Mailand and Dorothy Stites Alig, *Preserving Textiles: A Guide for the Nonspecialist* (Indianapolis: Indianapolis Museum of Art, 1999), 19.

2. Barbara Appelbaum, *Guide to Environmental Protection of Collections* (Madison, CT: Sound View Press, 1991), 112.

3. Mailand and Alig, *Preserving Textiles*, 38; Margaret T. Ordoñez, *Your Vintage Keepsake: A CSA Guide to Costume Storage and Display* (Lubbock: Texas Tech University Press, 2001), 11.

4. Mailand and Alig, *Preserving Textiles*, 37; Ordoñez, *Your Vintage Keepsake*, 12.

5. Ordoñez, *Your Vintage Keepsake*, 16.

6. Mailand and Alig, *Preserving Textiles*, 24–26.

7. Ibid., 29–30.

8. Appelbaum, *Guide to Environmental Protection of Collections*, 66–70.

9. Mailand and Alig, *Preserving Textiles*, 9.

10. Denise Dreher, *From the Neck Up: An Illustrated Guide to Hatmaking* (Minneapolis: Madhatter Press, 1981), 173, 176.

Bibliography

Oral Histories Appearing in Chapter 10

Julia Brazil, interview by author, April 7, 2004, Lufkin, Texas.
Faye Rusk, interview by author, April 6, 2004, Nacogdoches, Texas.
Louise Jenkins Rusk, interview by author, April 9, 2004, Lufkin, Texas.
Minnie Lee Skelton, interview by author, April 7, 2004, Lufkin, Texas.

The oral histories published in this volume have been transcribed by the author. Transcripts and original interview tapes are housed at the Gladys Marcus Library Special Collections, Fashion Institute of Technology, New York City.

Other Oral Histories

Johnson, Eileen. Sunbonnet maker and seller, Nacogdoches Trade Days
    flea market. Interview by author, January 4, 2004, Nacogdoches,
    Texas.
Louise Jenkins Rusk, interview by author, January 1, 2004, Lufkin, Texas.

Primary Sources

Boyd, Pearl Lowe. "From My Kitchen Window" column. *The Dunedin Times*. Dunedin, FL. 1950. In *Sunbonnets and Sweet Gum*, ed. Pearl Lowe Boyd and John Allen Boyd, 10–12. Philadelphia: by the author via Xlibris, 2001.

E. Butterick & Co's Summer Catalogue 1882. New York: Butterick, 1882. In *American Dress Pattern Catalogues, 1873–1909*, ed. Nancy Villa Bryk, 37–72. New York: Dover, 1988.

Caldwell, Erskine. *Tobacco Road*. Athens: University of Georgia Press, 1995.

Castillo, Ana. *My Father Was a Toltec and Selected Poems*. New York: Norton, 1995.

Cather, Willa. *O Pioneers!* New York: Barnes and Noble Classics, 2003.

Draper, Dorothy. *Entertaining Is Fun!: How to Be a Popular Hostess*. New York: Rizzoli, 2004.

Duff Gordon, Lady [Lucy]. *Discretions and Indiscretions*. London: Jarrolds, 1932.

Gaskell, Elizabeth. *Cranford*. London: Penguin Books, 1986.

"Hair Cut on 'Bias' Marks Daché Look." *New York Times*, July 15, 1958.

Harris, Dilue Rose. "Dilue Rose Harris." In *Texas Tears and Texas Sunshine: Voices of Frontier Women*, ed. Jo Ella Powell Exley, 53–74. College Station: Texas A&M University Press, 1985.

Jumper, Betty. Electronic mail to author, dated Monday, October 6, 2003.

Montgomery, Lucy Maud. *Anne of the Island*. Philadelphia: Running Press, 1997.

Pope, Virginia. "Lilly Daché Puts New Theory on Dressing into Her Exhibit." *New York Times*, September 23, 1954.

"Roadside Holiday, U.S.A." *Vogue* (March 1, 1954): 152–153.

Rodriguez, Richard. *Hunger of Memory: The Education of Richard Rodriguez*. New York: Bantam, 1982.

Stimpson, Eddie, Jr. *My Remembers: A Black Sharecropper's Recollections* of the Depression. Denton: University of North Texas Press, 1996.

Stryker, Ray Emerson, and Nancy Wood. *In This Proud Land: America 1935–1943 as Seen in the FSA Photographs.* New York: Galahad, 1973.

Thompson, Joanne W. Home economist. Letter to author, dated June 2004.

Twain, Mark. *Adventures of Huckleberry Finn.* New York: Harper & Row, 1987.

United Pentecostal Church International. "The Scriptures Decree Modesty in Dress." http://www.upci.org/doctrine/scripturesModesty.asp (accessed October 12, 2007).

Veblen, Thorstein. *The Theory of the Leisure Class.* New York: Dover, 1994.

"The Vogue of the Sunbonnet." *New York Times,* June 21, 1903.

Wilder, Laura Ingalls. *Little House on the Prairie.* New York: Harper Trophy, 1971.

Woman's Institute of Domestic Arts and Sciences, Ltd. *Fancy Aprons and Sunbonnets.* London: International Educational Publishing Company, 1916.

Youngblood, Mrs. Odell. "Sunbonnets." In *The Loblolly Book: Water Witching, Wild Hog Hunting, Home Remedies, Grandma's Moral Tales and Other Affairs of Plain Texas Living,* ed. Thad Sitton, 74. Austin: Texas Monthly Press, 1983.

Youngblood, Mrs. Ruby. "Sunbonnets." In *The Loblolly Book: Water Witching, Wild Hog Hunting, Home Remedies, Grandma's Moral Tales and Other Affairs of Plain Texas Living,* ed. Thad Sitton, 75. Austin, TX: Texas Monthly Press, 1983.

Secondary Sources

Appelbaum, Barbara. *Guide to Environmental Protection of Collections.* Madison, CT: Sound View Press, 1991.

Amphlett, Hilda. *Hats: A History of Fashion in Headwear.* Mineola, NY: Dover, 2003.

Bibliography

Aranda, José F., Jr. *When We Arrive: A New Literary History of Mexican America.* Tucson: University of Arizona Press, 2003.

Baumgarten, Linda. *Eighteenth-Century Clothing at Williamsburg.* Williamsburg, VA: The Colonial Williamsburg Foundation, 2002.

———. *What Clothes Reveal: The Language of Clothing in Colonial and Federal America.* New Haven, CT: The Colonial Williamsburg Foundation and Yale University Press, 2002.

Bissonette, Anne. *Early Neoclassical Hairstyles: 1750–1790.* Paper presented as part of the symposium "The Many Layered Meanings of Costume" at the annual meeting of the Costume Society of America Southeast Region, Williamsburg, VA, October 31–November 2, 2008.

Bolton, Andrew. *Men in Skirts.* London: V&A Publications, 2003.

Bowles, Hamish. *Jacqueline Kennedy: The White House Years.* New York: The Metropolitan Museum of Art and Bulfinch, 2001.

Callahan, Betty. "Make Your Own Sunbonnet . . . in Less than Two Hours." *Mother Earth News: The Original Guide to Living Wisely,* July/August 1978, online article archive, www.motherearthnews.com/DIY/1978-07 -01/Make-Your-Own-Sunbonnet-in-Less-Than-Two-Hours.aspx (accessed October 16, 2007).

Charles-Roux, Edmonde. *Chanel and Her World.* New York: Vendome, 1981.

Cheney, Joyce. *Aprons: Icons of the American Home.* Philadelphia: Running Press, 2000.

Clark, Fiona. *Hats.* London: Batsford, 1982.

Corfield, Penelope J. "Dress for Deference and Dissent: Hats and the Decline of Hat Honor," *Costume* 23 (1989): 71.

Cunnington, C. Willett, Phillis Cunnington, and Charles Beard. *A Dictionary of English Costume.* London: Adam and Charles Black, 1960.

236

De Courtais, Georgine. *Women's Headdresses and Hairstyles in England from AD 600 to the Present Day*. London: Batsford, 1986.

De Marly, Diana. *Working Dress: A History of Occupational Clothing*. New York: Holmes & Meier, 1986.

De Pauw, Linda Grant, and Conover Hunt. *"Remember the Ladies": Women in America, 1750–1815*. New York: Viking, 1976.

Dreher, Denise. *From the Neck Up: An Illustrated Guide to Hatmaking*. Minneapolis, MN: Madhatter Press, 1981.

Earnshaw, Pat. *A Dictionary of Lace*. Mineola, NY: Dover, 1999.

Etherington-Smith, Meredith, and Jeremy Pilcher. *The "It" Girls: Elinor Glyn, Novelist, and Her Sister Lucile, Couturière*. New York: Harcourt Brace Jovanovich, 1986.

Evans, George Ewart. "Dress and the Rural Historian." *Costume* 8 (1974): 38–40.

Ewing, George. "Forked Stick Folkcraft." In *Corners of Texas*, ed. Francis Edward Abernethy. Publication of the Texas Folklore Society LII, 105–113. Denton: University of North Texas Press, 1993.

ffolliott, Sheila. "Learning to Be Looked At: A Portrait of (the Artist as) a Young Woman in Agnès Merlet's *Artemisia*." In *Reclaiming Female Agency: Feminist Art History after Postmodernism*, ed. Norma Broude and Mary D. Garrard, 48–61. Berkeley: University of California Press, 2005.

Fischer, David Hackett. *Albion's Seed: Four British Folkways in America*. New York and Oxford: Oxford University Press, 1989.

Flanders, Judith. *Inside the Victorian Home: A Portrait of Domestic Life in Victorian England*. New York: Norton, 2004.

Font, Lourdes M., and Trudie A. Grace. *The Gilded Age: High Fashion and Society in the Hudson Highlands, 1865–1914*. Cold Spring, NY: Putnam County Historical Society & Foundry School Museum, 2006.

Bibliography

Foster, Helen Bradley. *"New Raiments of Self": African American Clothing in the Antebellum South*. Oxford: Berg, 1997.

Friedman, Lawrence M. *The History of American Law*. New York: Touchstone, 1985.

Gabler, Neal. *Walt Disney: The Triumph of American Imagination*. New York: Alfred A. Knopf, 2006.

Hall, Carrie A., and Rose G. Kretsinger. *The Romance of the Patchwork Quilt in America*. New York: Bonanza, 1935.

Helvenston, Sally I. "Fashion and Function in Women's Dress in Rural New England: 1840–1900." *Dress* 18 (1991): 26–38.

Hollander, Anne. *Seeing Through Clothes*. Berkeley: University of California Press, 1993.

"How to Sew a Sunbonnet." www.ehow.com/how_2077833 _sew-sunbonnet.html (accessed October 16, 2007).

Ierley, Merritt. *The Comforts of Home: The American House and the Evolution of Modern Convenience*. New York: Three Rivers, 1999.

Illinois State Museum. *At Home in a House Divided: 1850–1880*. December 31, 1996. www.museum.state.il.us/exhibits/athome/1850/objects/sad iron.htm (accessed October 13, 2007).

Jeffery, Janet K. "The Sunbonnet as Folk Costume." In *Corners of Texas*, ed. Francis Edward Abernethy. Publication of the Texas Folklore Society LII, 208–219. Denton: University of North Texas Press, 1993.

Jensen, Joan M. *With These Hands: Women Working on the Land*. Old Westbury, NY: The Feminist Press/McGraw-Hill, 1981.

Jones, Terri. "Sunbonnets." *Bittersweet* IV, no. 4 (Summer 1977): 25–30.

Kiracofe, Roderick, and Mary Elizabeth Johnson. *The American Quilt: A History of Cloth and Comfort, 1750–1950*. New York: Clarkson Potter, 1993.

Lester, Katherine M., and Rose N. Kerr. *Historic Costume*. Peoria, IL: Bennett, 1977.

Mackenzie, Althea. *Buttons and Trimmings*. London: The National Trust, 2004.

Mailand, Harold F., and Dorothy Stites Alig. *Preserving Textiles: A Guide for the Nonspecialist*. Indianapolis: Indianapolis Museum of Art, 1999.

Martin, Richard. *Our New Clothes: Acquisitions of the 1990s*. New York: The Metropolitan Museum of Art, 1999.

Milbank, Caroline Rennolds. *New York Fashion: The Evolution of American Style*. New York: Abrams, 1989.

Mills, Betty J. *Calico Chronicle*. Lubbock: Texas Tech University Press, 1985.

Ordoñez, Margaret T. *Your Vintage Keepsake: A CSA Guide to Costume Storage and Display*. Lubbock: Texas Tech University Press, 2001.

Perrot, Philippe. *Fashioning the Bourgeoisie: A History of Clothing in the Nineteenth Century*. Trans. Richard Bienvenu. Princeton, NJ: Princeton University Press, 1994.

Prown, Jules David. "The Truth of Material Culture: History or Fiction?" In *History from Things: Essays on Material Culture*, ed. Steven Lubar and W. David Kingery, 1–19. Washington, DC: Smithsonian Institution Press, 1995.

Ribeiro, Aileen. *Dress and Morality*. Oxford: Berg, 2003.

———. *Fashion and Fiction: Dress in Art and Literature in Stuart England*. New Haven, CT: Yale University Press, 2005.

Ritchie, Donald A. *Doing Oral History*. New York: Twayne Publishers, 1995. [Appendix includes "Principles and Standards of the Oral History Association."]

Schultz, Clarence C. "Whatever Happened to the Little Frame House on the Prairie?" In *Texas Country: The Changing Rural Scene*, ed. Glen E. Lich and Dona B. Reeves-Marquardt, 93–116. College Station: Texas A&M University Press, 1986.

Schlereth, Thomas J., ed. *Material Culture: A Research Guide*. Lawrence: University Press of Kansas, 1985.

Schlesinger, Arthur Meier. *The Rise of the City 1878–1898*. With an introduction by Andrea Tuttle Kornbluh. Columbus: Ohio State University Press, 1999.

Severa, Joan. *Dressed for the Photographer: Ordinary Americans and Fashion, 1840–1900*. Kent, OH, and London: Kent State University Press, 1995.

Smallwood, J. B., Jr. "Cotton, Cattle, and Crude: The Texas Economy, 1865–1980." In *Texas Country: The Changing Rural Scene*, ed. Glen E. Lich and Dona B. Reeves-Marquardt, 67–91. College Station: Texas A&M University Press, 1986.

Smith, Tumbleweed. *Under the Chinaberry Tree*. Austin: Eakin Press, 2002.

Strawn, Susan, Jane Farrell-Beck, and Ann R. Hemken. "Bib Overalls: Function and Fashion." *Dress* 32 (2005): 43–55.

Tademy, Lalita. *Cane River*. New York: Warner Books, 2001.

Tandberg, Gerilyn. "Confederate Bonnets: Imagination and Ingenuity." *Dress* 32 (2005): 14–26.

West, Elliott. *Growing Up with the Country: Childhood on the Far Western Frontier*. Albuquerque: University of New Mexico Press, 1989.

Wilcox, R. Turner. *The Mode in Hats and Headdresses*. New York: Scribner's, 1945.

Williamson, Samuel H. "An Index of the Wage of Unskilled Labor from 1774 to the Present." Economic History Services, December 2004. http://www.eh.net/hmit/databases/unskilledwage (accessed November 11, 2008).

Tortora, Phyllis G., ed. *Fairchild's Dictionary of Textiles*, 7th ed. New York: Fairchild, 2000.

Wiley, Bell Irwin. *Confederate Women: Beyond the Petticoat*. New York: Barnes and Noble, 1994.

Wollen, Peter. *Raiding the Icebox: Reflections on Twentieth-Century Culture*. Bloomington and Indianapolis: University of Indiana Press, 1993.

Index

Index

Index

Index

Index

Index